Praise for *Homeschoolers*

"Filled with encouragement for new hom
tips on how to get started, *Homeschoolers A   ...ⁱⁱˢ is a useful
handbook for those interested in getting started with secular homeschooling. By sharing her experience and personal perspective as a
homeschooling parent, Oaks offers a model for homeschooling that
is flexible, fun, and worry-free." – Rachel Gathercole, Author of *The
Well-Adjusted Child*

"I LOVE LOVE LOVE this book. It's an easy read. It's engaging.
It's inspirational. It puts homeschooling in historical context, which
I did not expect and knew very little about. As an educator and
someone who knows people currently homeschooling I can think of
so many people who would get so much from this book. I am going
to share this book widely!" – Ellen Rondina, Author of *Self-Care
Revolution*

"Kathy Oaks writes a clear, detailed narrative of her and her family's
journey from conventional schoolers to unconventional learners. Her
suggestions and ideas for helping children learn at home in their own
ways and for parents struggling with criticism for homeschooling
their children will give you confidence and direction to live and learn
well with your children." – Patrick Farenga, Publisher, John Holt/
Growing Without Schooling LLC

"This fun and educational book takes homeschooling myths and
turns them on their heads. Learning doesn't have to be hard, and
homeschooling doesn't have to be sitting around a table for hours
working on a boxed curriculum. Take a look at *Homeschoolers Are Not
Hermits* to see how to bring play and fun to your homeschool day,
with plenty of time to be social." – Kytka Hilmar-Jezek, Author of *99
Questions and Answers about Unschooling*

Homeschoolers Are Not Hermits

A Practical Guide to Raising Smart, Confident, and Socially Connected Kids

Kathy Oaks

Homeschoolers Are Not Hermits: A Practical Guide to Raising Smart, Confident, and Socially Connected Kids

Copyright © 2018 by Kathy Oaks
Published by Kathy Oaks
Printed by IngramSpark, first printing Nov. 2018
ISBN: 978-1-7322731-0-8
Cover Design: Patti Knoles
Editor: Karl Monger
Interior Design: Charlie Chauvin

A Note to the Reader: Every effort has been made to ensure that the information contained in this book is complete and accurate. However, this book is intended to be educational and of a general nature. It does not constitute therapeutic or other professional advice for any specific individual or situation, including the choice to begin homeschooling or any type of therapy. The author and publisher are in no way liable for any misuse of this material.

Acknowledgements: The author would like to thank Alfie Kohn, Patrick Farenga, Dr. David Walsh, Dr. Peter Gray, Rachel Gathercole, Pattie Fitzgerald, Dr. Howard Gardner, Kytka Hilmar-Jezek, Kim Jaworski, Alyson Long, Vivek Patel, Aza Donnelly, Susie Zahratka and Dori Moss for permission to use their material, and for being an inspiration to me along my parenting and homeschooling journey.

CONTENTS

Introduction

How did two people who were such good students become homeschoolers?

People often ask me about my choice to homeschool, baffled because my husband Tom and I both did well in a traditional school setting. We were the kind of students that teachers dream of: quiet and well behaved, always on top of our homework, and happy to answer that one question that stumps everyone else. We both went to university on scholarship, and my husband went on to get his Ph.D. and two post-docs in chemistry before becoming a professor himself.

So what changed us from good little students to parents who chose to go outside the mainstream of education? (Granted, homeschooling is not quite so fringe these days as it once was.)

Having always been interested in how people work, when our first child was an infant I found myself devouring books on child development. I wanted to know everything there was to know and do the very best for him. It was around that time that I had a moment of epiphany, not about homeschooling, but about raising our children. It was a beautiful day, and the sun was streaming into our bedroom. My baby was lying on our bed and I was making those silly faces at him when I realized that THIS was why I had a psychology degree, this moment right here and all the moments yet to come. This was what my interest in brain development and bonding and learning was all about: helping my son become the best person he could be. What better purpose could there be?

Always eager to learn, I looked for more books about learning and development. In 2004, books were the way to go—there weren't a lot of online resources yet. I was considering numerous suggestions I'd found in the Amazon reviews. One of those suggestions led me to John Taylor Gatto's 1990 acceptance speech for New York City Teacher of the Year award, which is now available in a book of essays titled, *Dumbing Us Down*. It completely changed the way I looked at my experiences in school. I remember generally having good memories of school and learning, and that everything else was a product of the time, the place, or the other kids. Gatto's speech motivated me to look at the structure and purpose of the educational system itself. When I did, I realized for the first time how often I had been molded to fit into that system and how it had shaped the way I looked at my own capacity for learning, for setting and achieving my own goals rather than those set by others. I could see myself, in retrospect, being stunted, adjusting my dreams to fit what might be accomplished by going to college and getting a "good job." I loved taking art and photography classes, but I never thought this passion could be my job. It took the derailment of my post-graduate plans and expectations to shake me up enough to look at the possibility of actually being a photographer.

I don't want that for our kids. I want them to reach for the stars and go after what most inspires them.

When I discussed the possibility of homeschooling with Tom I discovered that he had been bullied in school for being so smart and not particularly athletic. He was willing to try any plan that would spare our kids that kind of experience, and he trusted me to pick the best path for our family. So we decided to homeschool and jumped right in, first with one son and now with three.

TOM SAYS: I felt like, for me, being successful at school didn't prepare me to be successful at life. At school there are clear goals set by others, and I enjoyed accomplishing them, but school does not teach how to choose your own goals. Life does not give you specific objectives to pursue; you must create and pursue them yourself. At first, I wasn't in favor of homeschooling, per se, but I wasn't against it either. I got some flak for "letting" Kathy homeschool the boys, but I trusted her implicitly and I could see that she had lots of good ideas and that the boys were flourishing.

A little about our family

My husband Tom and I have three boys, now ages 6-14, who are interested in learning about a wide variety of things. In fact, we as a family are constantly learning new things! I grew up as a (fairly) well-behaved straight-A student with a love of art, photography, and human behavior. Both of my parents are university professors and are the ones who fostered a love of learning in me and my brother. They tried hard to encourage us to find things we had a passion for and then figure out how to make a living doing them. It took me a little while to shake off the constraints of school and follow that advice. I have a degree in psychology and have worked as a teacher in the states and in Japan. My main profession, photography, is on hold while I devote my time to our family and community. My husband is a university chemistry professor who also teaches classes for homeschoolers in chemistry and physics. In his spare time he enjoys woodworking, designs and builds airplanes and architectural models from Lego, and reads about aerodynamics.

Why I wrote this book

I decided to write about our experience because so many people have helped our family along our homeschooling journey, and because whenever I meet someone just beginning the process I want to help them, too. And not only beginning homeschoolers. I love knowing that I've made a difference, even if it's just a little bit. I find myself jumping in to online conversations to add my two cents, and if I had the time (and they had the patience) I would easily make it my two dollars. It feels like I can't help enough. I always want to hold people's hands along the way and reassure them that it's not nearly as big and scary and complicated as it may seem at the start.

Then it occurred to me that I could write it all down in one place, all the advice and experience and resources that have helped me, and in this way help other people. Those just starting out on the homeschooling journey have more immediate questions and fears than those farther along, but I have found that no matter how many years of homeschooling experience any of us have, we can always learn more from each other and contribute a little something as well.

Another reason I wrote this book is to counteract a lot of false ideas people have about homeschooling, many of which keep people from seeing it as a viable option for themselves . I can't tell you how many times I've heard, "I'd love to homeschool, but my child is so *social!*" Homeschooling doesn't have to be school-at-home. It doesn't look like a mini-classroom with desks and children doing workbooks and the parent lecturing at the front of the room for eight hours. That would be boring and tedious and hard and stressful for kids and parents alike. Homeschooling also does not have to stunt your family socially, unless you absolutely insist on school-at-home with no extra-curricular activities. That's right, *homeschoolers are not hermits.* Bear in mind that until about 200 years ago, the vast majority of humanity was well-socialized without school, and even when compulsory schooling arrived it didn't require the huge amount of time (and homework) that it does today. Education does not have to take up 30-60 hours a week for 12-16 years, nor does it require that children memorize a bunch of facts just so they can regurgitate them on a test. Learning can and should be enjoyable, and it can look however your family wants it to look. If your kids really want to do workbooks for eight hours a day, then let them try it for a day or two. Just make sure you don't force them into it, and that you take a break from it and get them out of the house for some fun on a regular basis. Helping children learn how to reason, to think critically, and to put together facts to create new ideas and concepts makes learning fun.

Also, there seem to be fewer books (and sites and groups) for secular homeschoolers than there are for those who identify religion as their main reason for homeschooling. I don't mean to imply this book is intended only for people who are non-religious. What I mean is that religion is not brought into the equation. This is the only place it will be mentioned, because that's not what our homeschooling education is about. Our spiritual practices are separate from our educational practices, and that is intentional. We prefer to expose our kids to a variety of beliefs, and discuss them as they are relevant to other people's lives and our own. One of my homeschooling friends summed it up like this: "I pray with my prayer group, I come to get homeschool support in my homeschooling group." We are ethics- and science-based homeschoolers. If you would like to read books on how to incorporate your spiritual practice into your daily education, there are plenty to choose from. This book was written, in part, as a secular alternative. As a side note, when I say there are plenty of books on spirituality and religion, I do mean plenty. In a bookstore once I found a book titled *Pagan Homeschooling*. Sure enough, it was all about how to incorporate pagan spiritual practice into your daily homeschooling life. Naturally, your spiritual side may inform your life, but that is personal, and beliefs vary widely among people. In this book I do not presume to tell you how to meld your spiritual practices with your education.

Finally, a lot of this book has to do with our parenting style. Because our kids are at home with us so much of the time, it's hard to avoid the subject. Our goal is to help our kids to become self-sufficient, creative, interesting, kind, mindful, giving, and effective members of society. It's not to make them obedient or to protect them from ideas (although protecting them from mean people is right up there on our list). We strive for respectful and cooperative parenting, although we often fall back on authoritative (as opposed to authoritarian) parenting when at a loss. One of my goals in writing this is to show you that nobody is perfect, that it's natural to make mistakes along the way, and that the best approach is always to relax and deal with the issue calmly. Don't waste time beating yourself up for making mistakes. We all make mistakes. What has worked well for our family is to be mindful when problems arise, discuss the problem together, and all brainstorm for solutions. Remember, most of the stories you read from homeschoolers are about their best days, not their worst. Homeschoolers generally save their bad day stories to share with their support groups, not to publish on a blog. It's getting a lot better, but there are still plenty of people who are ready to jump on you and tell you to send your kids to public school if you even hint at admitting that homeschooling is less than perfect.

What will you get out of reading this book?

My hope is that I can intersperse practical advice with enough insight into our homeschool lives (and those of our friends) that I can ease your concerns and help you become confident about your family's educational choices. This book is all about helping homeschooling families to relax, build stronger bonds with one another, and learn to enjoy learning together.

I begin with the most basic questions and proceed from there. Feel free to read this straight through or go right to the section that interests you most. I've also included short tips at the end of each section so that you can come back for a quick brush-up without having to read the whole section all over again. I am also listing the resources and references at the end of each chapter so that you don't have to wait until the end of the book to locate useful information.

My husband Tom has interspersed his thoughts throughout the book in the hopes that another point of view might help clarify or deepen your understanding.

What won't you get out of reading this book?

This book will not turn your family into the perfect homeschooling family. The reason for that is simple. That family doesn't exist! Reading it won't turn your children into well-mannered, overachieving geniuses or you into the world's most patient and brilliant teacher. You *may* become more patient, and your children *may* decide you are brilliant, provided this book helps you feel confident enough to work together to figure out what homeschooling will look like for your family.

This book is also not a giant compendium of homeschooling resources and ideas for you to refer to on a daily basis. There are plenty of other books that do that, and there is no need for me to reinvent the wheel. I have still included plenty of useful books in the resources sections. Look them up, check them out at your library, and pick a few favorites to buy and keep on the shelf. In fact, keep books of homeschooling ideas on a low shelf where the kids can read them. Mine like to browse through ours regularly when they are looking for something to do, which leads them to fun and interesting activities they get to choose themselves. Self-motivation is big in our house.

Lastly, this book is not here to tell you that you're doing it all wrong. You've already been doing a great job, especially if you're the kind of parent who cares enough about your child's education to actually read a book like this. If this book can give you even one idea or tip that will make your job easier, more fun, and more relaxed, then it has done its job.

Dumbing Us Down

What follows is summary of high school teacher John Taylor Gatto's famous essay and speech, delivered when he was named the 1990 New York City Teacher of the Year.

What he really teaches in school:

1. **Confusion:** He teaches too many facts and too many subjects that must be memorized, all without context. Adjectives, architectural drawing, the orbiting of planets, slavery, the law of large numbers, assemblies, et cetera.

2. **Class Position:** If he does his job well, no student will be able to imagine belonging to another social class. They will fear and envy the upper classes and hold lower ones in contempt.

3. **Indifference:** Students will learn through competing for the teacher's attention that only what is included in the lessons matters; all else is incidental and unimportant. Interest in the subject beyond the lesson is discouraged, as is interest in other subjects not covered.

4. **Emotional Dependency:** He teaches through stars, checks, smiles, frowns, prizes and punishments that students must depend on him for how they feel, that he is the authority who can grant them any rights they have in a school. There is no free speech or thought or individuality in school except that granted by authority.

5. **Intellectual Dependency:** The students must wait to be told what to learn, what lessons to do, and then do it to his satisfaction. Students learn to wait for other people, those trained and in authority, to direct them in life and give their lives meaning.

They should not take any initiative except within strictly defined boundaries.

6. **Provisional Self-Esteem:** He teaches that a student's self-respect depends on expert opinion, on external factors like tests, grades, and report cards instead of one's sense of self. Students need to learn to be told what they are worth.

7. **One Can't Hide:** Students learn they are always watched. There is no private time, in fact no privacy at school, and each student learns to fear punishment if they do not behave appropriately. There is no chance to learn anything other than what is taught. Homework is assigned to restrict the students' time at home, to extend this watching into the community so there is little chance of learning something other than these seven lessons.

Dumbing Us Down, John Taylor Gatto, New Society Publishers Anniversary Edition, June 13, 2017

Getting Started

Why do people homeschool?

"Do not yearn to be popular; be exquisite. Do not desire to be famous; be loved. Do not take pride in being expected; be palpable, unmistakable."

– C. JOYBELL C.

"A community is composed of its citizens, so what is good for the children is ultimately good for the community as well... parents who are good citizens will raise kids who are good citizens regardless of where they go to school."

– RACHEL GATHERCOLE, *THE WELL-ADJUSTED CHILD*

What are the reasons that people homeschool? They are many and varied, but at the bottom the reasons all boil down to one: we want our children to thrive. Some people homeschool because they have so enjoyed watching their children grow and learn as babies and toddlers that they want to continue through the school age years. Some people have looked at the science of learning and seen that the current educational system is too rigid to incorporate most of the things that would actually be effective. Some people have had bad experiences themselves in the school system and don't want their children to be subjected to those same experiences. Some people have been teachers and love to teach. More and more, though, people who homeschool are trying compulsory schooling, seeing that it fails for one or more of their children, and are pulling them out to homeschool. Below are some of the benefits of homeschooling.

The benefits of homeschooling fall into four main areas, and some of the benefits apply to the whole family and not just the individual students:

- ability to tailor the education to fit the student
- freedom and flexibility
- social and emotional health
- physical and mental health
- fostering critical thinking

Many of the benefits of homeschooling will be touched on throughout the book, such as positive socialization with people of all ages and the ability to tailor each child's education to their individual learning styles and interests. This is just a brief synopsis of some of the biggest perks of homeschooling.

Tailoring education

Being able to tailor your kids' education individually is a priceless, if time-consuming, benefit. Our kids are so different from one another in terms of their personalities, needs, and learning styles. Most people have multiple areas of intelligence and use more than one learning style. School mainly works well for those with strengths in only two of the eight areas of intelligence and two of the learning styles, which I cover in chapter five. Homeschooling allows students to expand any of those areas rather than focusing on developing only those that will enable them to do well in a traditional school setting.

Learning in context and making connections is one major benefit of homeschooling. The parent is there through all the years, from birth to graduation. This means that you're able to connect something you're learning about this year to what was learned last year, or the year before. And not just with curriculum, but with everyday things. We went on a road trip to see the grandparents, during which we visited two of the Great Lakes. Next time we are reading about geography or history or the ecology of waterways, I can mention our Great Lakes trip. A quick reminder that this applies to something they've experienced goes a very long way toward making it more relevant and meaningful. They can put an image to a place on a map, compare the clean beaches to photos of the pollution of fifty years ago, or imagine the sturgeon swimming in those vast waters.

Connections

Contextual connections happen for us on a regular basis. In the movie *Hidden Figures* the mathematician Euler is mentioned. I told our oldest that his dad has some books on Euler and pulled one out for him. He loved it, and that started him working his way through his dad's math shelf. Recently we were looking through some old *Muse* magazines, and we came across an article about a cave in Mexico that contained the world's largest gypsum crystals. The kids got to dig up some gypsum crystals with their geologist grandfather at the Great Salt Lake last year, and I reminded them that those were the same kind of crystals. Another time we found strange tracks in the mud in Colorado, and the next day we found a match for them in a nature center - bear tracks!

These are just a few instances that come to mind. It's the ability to make these kinds of connections that makes homeschooling so wonderful, and so rich in learning and in understanding the world around us. There is no way that a schoolteacher could know anything about the individual experiences that students have had in prior years, either in class or at home, beyond the basics. As a family, you have a giant advantage. And it's not just the parents, either. I have heard our sons sharing things with one another, explaining and remembering and having "Aha!" moments among themselves, and reminding us of things that we've experienced that connect current learning with past events.

Efficiency is another benefit of individual education. A lot of new homeschoolers, and plenty of veterans, wonder if they are really doing enough work because covering the material doesn't take as long as they were expecting. If it takes eight hours in school, why doesn't it take that long at home? There are lots of reasons to account for this: less time wasted getting everyone up to speed after each break, using the right materials and/or learning styles for each child, learning at their own best pace instead of having to slow down or keep up with the group, learning when they are most alert, following their natural interests, being able to put their learning into context, and taking plenty of breaks.

Making mistakes can be a great way to learn, once mistakes are not seen as bad things. School does not encourage making mistakes, but homeschoolers can build it into their curriculum if they want to. Not being afraid to make mistakes, and then learning from them, can lead to insights that stick around and to innovations that can benefit others. "I make more mistakes than anyone else I know. And, sooner or later, I patent most of them." - Thomas Edison, 1847-1931, inventor and businessman.

As a bonus, we parents get to expand our knowledge of the world, too. Whenever a new interest comes around, often the whole family learns something about it, either through books or videos or through discussing it at the table and doing hands-on projects. I have learned about things I never knew before and deepened my knowledge of other subjects.

Freedom and flexibility

The freedom and flexibility to pursue our interests is a big benefit of homeschooling in our family. It means that if there is a subject we want to delve deeper into, we have the time (and flexibility) to do so. Or, if there is a subject that we need to spend extra time on because we're not understanding it, we can stop and take that time. If something is boring we don't have to just push through it, we can figure out why it's boring and fix it. Maybe it's too easy or too repetitive, or maybe there's a more interesting book or video that we could switch to.

Flexibility is available not just in how much time to spend on a subject, but in a number of other areas as well. Our oldest can work on both advanced math and remedial spelling, and our middle son can enjoy reading several grade levels ahead while working right on grade level for math. Scheduling is also flexible, as is the environment. Different times of day and different physical locations work best for different kids. It's not just about the kids, though. There is more flexibility for the parents, as well. Some people take their kids to the office with them, while others teach their kids at home in the evening after work. Five years ago I couldn't imagine bringing our boys to work, but now our oldest two would do fine provided they had enough to occupy themselves.

There is a lot of freedom in homeschooling, and not just to pursue our own interests and go at our own pace. There is the freedom to choose any curriculum, or none at all. (Some states are picky about this, though, and I have known families to move across state lines to free them from a set curriculum.) There is freedom to go to the restroom or get a drink of water whenever you need to, kids and adults alike. Freedom to ask questions about any material at almost any time (when mom is cooking is not the best time to ask complicated math questions) rather than waiting to be called on and being confined to the subject at hand. Freedom to pursue a subject beyond the curriculum, and beyond book learning. Freedom to change the schedule to allow more time for interest-led learning. Freedom to pause a lesson and come back to it another time. Freedom to go outside when it's a nice day, to learn outside or just blow off schoolwork and hike in the woods instead. Freedom to take vacations when everyone else is in school.

There is also freedom from spending long hours in school. The amount of time we need to devote to education is so much less than the time they would be in school that we have a big chunk of time left to work on everything else. Our oldest son can practice piano and read math books for fun while other kids slog through worksheets. Our middle son can create board games and costumes for plays while other kids raise their hands and wait to be called on. Our youngest son can work on building electrical circuits while other kids wait for the school bus, not because it's in the curriculum of a kindergartener, but because learning with ease and play leaves so much time for other pursuits. I very much enjoy the freedom from trying to fit in to a fairly inflexible system.

Social and emotional health
Contrary to popular belief, positive socialization can be a big benefit

of homeschooling. There is more time to spend interacting freely with peers, as opposed to sitting next to them quietly in a classroom. There is closer individual supervision by adults who can redirect behavior into positive channels. There is a wider age range of children and adults to interact with on a regular basis. There is more time to form close friendships and more time to form close bonds with family members. Seeking out homeschool groups and spending more time supervising group and family interaction is definitely more work than sending the kids off to school, but the benefits can greatly outweigh the time spent in terms of raising socially adept kids.

Many people are concerned that homeschooled children won't become the "good citizens" that going to school would have led them to be. In fact, if you look at the actual numbers you find the opposite is true. Homeschoolers are more likely to be involved in their communities, more likely to vote, and more likely to donate to causes they care about, as referenced in *The Well-Adjusted Child*, by Rachel Gathercole. And on the subject of turning their backs on the school system, those who homeschool still pay taxes. That means that for every 30 students who are homeschooled the public school budget gets a whole classroom's worth of monetary resources that can then be provided to students and teachers who need them. It may not go to the specific school that your child would have gone to, and if you think it should then consider getting involved in your local school board politics.

Another major benefit of homeschooling is the general lack of peer pressure and bullying, provided you don't settle for joining a group that ends up being rigid and inflexible. Because homeschoolers are much more influenced by their families and close friends than they are by school culture, there is a lot more freedom to think, act, and wear things that fall outside the narrow window of what is considered acceptable in school. This gives homeschoolers more leeway to make their own choices and feel more confident in those choices. People who are confident in themselves are less likely to pressure others to be like them out of insecurity, or, in turn to give in to pressure to conform even when that is undesirable. Homeschoolers already know that they are bucking the trend by not going to school, which can help build confidence in making choices that might challenge the status quo. It also helps to have a much higher adult-to-kid ratio, as long as the adults are paying attention to what is going on.

The Sparkle Pants

The first example that comes to mind when I think of peer pressure is that of the sparkle pants... One fine winter day our middle boy went out sledding with his friend, and as there had been a lot of freeze/thaw that year the two of them broke through into a big puddle and got soaked. They went back to her house for hot chocolate and a change of clothes, and he came home wearing a pair of jeans covered with sparkly gems. On our way to board game club that afternoon he realized that he was still wearing her pants, and he worried that people might give him a hard time. I coached him a bit on what to say so that he could pull it off with nonchalance if anyone teased him, but not one person did. In fact, he said later that nobody even mentioned it. It was such a non-issue that he didn't even remember wearing the pants to board game club when I asked him about it while writing this chapter. People felt free to wear whatever they wanted in that group, without being afraid their peers would tease them for it. Two kids even wore superhero costumes on a regular basis, just for fun, and one of the kids felt the freedom to make up her own original superhero, complete with costume.

I remember all the teasing I got as a kid whenever I wore unusual clothes. There was a woman who illustrated the most beautiful T-shirts for the American Mammal Society, and my mom always brought some home when she went to conferences. I learned to only wear them on weekends because I got teased unmercifully for wearing shirts with sea otters or fruit bats on them. It took a long time for me to break out of that mold and wear fun and unusual things again. It does my heart good to see our kids wearing things that express who they are (like math joke T-shirts and neon colors and fedoras) without being razzed by their peers. Moreover, they have the self-confidence to wear whatever they feel like because they were never subjected to the pressures of conformity that I was.

Another benefit of homeschooling is that families can foster competition or cooperation in whichever situations warrant them, rather than the constant competition of the classroom. Our oldest became highly competitive, and a sore loser, when he was early elementary age. I had seen the effects of that kind of attitude played out before, and we were able to work around it. We only played cooperative games for at least two years, until he was able to be a gracious winner and a good sport when he lost. Our household rule is that it's a good game to play as long as everybody is having a good time. If anyone stops having fun, even from just losing consistently, it's time to find a new game. That applies to any kind of game, as well as many situations in life, not just to board games.

One major benefit to homeschooling that helped to convince us to try it is the closeness it brings to siblings. The more I looked into it, the more I heard people talking about what great friends their kids had become. As we'll discuss in chapter three, the same definitely holds true for our family. There are certainly times when the kids want to do their own things and times I need to separate them, but they all get along pretty well, with our two oldest being quite close. There are many times that they will consult with each other before deciding whether to take a class or camp, because they want to be in it together.

A number of the benefits just listed can be lumped together under what I consider developing the whole child. We probably spend more time talking about personal interactions and modeling the kind of behavior we would like to see them use than we do working with them on academic studies. In the long run, we think that will serve them well.

Physical and mental health

Being cooped up all day is bad for your health. As homeschoolers you have the ability to exercise more often and go outside frequently, or even just get up out of your chairs and move around. One family we know takes a mile-long hike every day as part of their physical education, and another has formed a weekly outdoor games club to play organized games (like tag and capture the flag) with friends. As a bonus, staying home when you're sick is encouraged when you homeschool, and often it is a time when homeschoolers catch up on any schoolwork. For those with severe allergies, being able to control what comes into one's environment can be a game changer. If the group you're in isn't currently cognizant of health challenges, please bring it up and see if people will accommodate you.

Too much stress is also bad for your health. There is generally a lot less stress associated with homeschooling than with conventional school. A lot of school stress comes from both children and parents having little to no control over what happens during the school day and what homework needs to be completed afterwards. This is where flexibility and freedom come to the rescue. If you are using a curriculum that isn't working, change it. If you are in a social group or a class that it would be better to quit, you can quit. Working at your own pace in a flexible environment where mistakes are okay and busywork is unnecessary are all great for lowering stress, as is having support in social situations.

Homeschooling can also be helpful for those with anxiety, whether it is social anxiety or test anxiety or some other kind. It allows both parents and students the time to deal with issues without worrying about being late or missing school or having a teacher who doesn't understand. Homeschoolers can still experience anxiety, but having flexibility and a supportive environment can help mitigate the problems.

Fostering Critical Thinking

This benefit directly results from the other four benefits. While tailoring the education to fit each student, you can work with each to do much more than memorize and regurgitate answers. You can delve into the reasons behind things, understand how others see the world, and question whether there might be a better way, or a number of ways, to do something. There is more time to explore ideas and to answer questions because of the efficiency of homeschooling. Generating multiple working hypotheses helps students to be discerning about what is presented to them (especially online these days), and to be willing to challenge ideas, including their own. This will also enable them to develop objectivity and thoroughness and a willingness to consider the ideas of others. Learning things in context can help them tease out nuances and see what might not fit, or see a new way that concepts can go together. Valuing mistakes as learning opportunities encourages students to self-correct, and to dig deeper when they haven't understood something.

The freedom and flexibility to pursue what interests each individual also can lead to critical thinking skills, not only about a particular subject, but about oneself. Learning happens best when a person is engaged, interested and excited about a subject. This fosters self-motivation and a better understanding of oneself, one's interests, and one's capabilities. If you know you are able to buckle down and learn one thing quickly, or at least with dedication, then you know you can apply that ability to other subjects that you want to learn. Some subjects may come more easily than others, but knowing you've done it before and how you learn best will go a long way toward building the confidence to tackle any subject. This is critical thinking applied to one's own learning techniques.

Likewise, having good social and emotional health will go a long way toward understanding how to take care of your emotional needs and those of others, and understanding social dynamics. These subjects are rarely discussed in school, and the social dynamics learned there are often unhealthy. People mature emotionally at different rates in the same way they mature physically at different rates. Homeschooling allows parents to buffer their children from the worst effects of bullying and social exclusion while being on hand to model correct behavior and discuss the reasons why people should and shouldn't act in particular ways. Being able to analyze what's happening in a situation and then change the dynamic, and knowing when to get out of a bad situation, are great uses for critical thinking skills.

Finally, having both physical and mental health are certainly needed for critical thinking skills. It's hard to think clearly if you are tired, hungry, sick or in pain. Having to spend hours every day in school under any of those conditions because of an attendance requirement is counterproductive. Having a physical condition doesn't have to derail the educational process for homeschoolers. The ability to get learning done more quickly while homeschooling allows for plenty of time for rest and recuperation, not to mention getting enough sleep. Kids going through a growth spurt can eat as often as they need to, and learning can happen in ways that help make someone with pain or a disability as physically comfortable as possible. Mental health is another important component of thinking clearly. Anyone dealing with depression, anxiety, or other mentally debilitating conditions will be preoccupied to various degrees with keeping it together rather than focusing solely on education. The whole idea of daily forcing a child to go into a situation he or she is not yet emotionally or mentally equipped to handle should make it obvious why childhood depression and social anxiety are on the rise. Homeschoolers can create an environment that supports mental health as much as possible, which will facilitate the ability to think critically.

A Few Pros and Cons of Homeschooling

- ✔ **PRO:** You don't have to get up early to get kids out the door, and everyone gets enough sleep.
- ✗ **CON:** You don't have to get up early, so everyone gets up at a different time.

- ✔ **PRO:** You can stay in your pajamas all day if you really want to.
- ✗ **CON:** There's no motivation to get out of your pajamas if you don't have to go anywhere.

✔ **PRO:** Kids have more free time to play and be kids.

✘ **CON:** Parents lose the free time that their kids would otherwise be in school.

✔ **PRO:** You can tailor your homeschooling to fit the needs of each child.

✘ **CON:** Tailoring to each individual can be a lot of work, which is why schools don't do it.

✔ **PRO:** There is a lot less bullying and peer pressure.

✘ **CON:** You have to be ready to mediate, turning problem situations into learning experiences.

✔ **PRO:** Your kids will be more comfortable spending time around people of all ages.

✘ **CON:** Your kids will have fewer same-age peers, although not necessarily fewer good friends.

✔ **PRO:** No school fundraisers.

✘ **CON:** It's harder to participate in band, orchestra, team sports, and school trips.

Finally, remember that homeschooling does not guarantee any of these advantages, it only offers the opportunity. If you stick rigidly to a school-at-home curriculum and atmosphere, you will still be a homeschooler, but you will miss out on many of the benefits of flexibility, freedom, and tailoring the education to your kids. On the other hand, it may cause you less stress than finding (and paying for) just the right curriculum for each child, or worrying that not following a curriculum at all will put your kids at a disadvantage. Homeschooling may give your children more time to explore their strengths and interests, but it won't necessarily turn them into geniuses or musical prodigies. Homeschooling may bring family members closer together, but there may always be friction between particular members of your family. Conversely, sending your kids to school will not automatically ruin them for life. Plenty of people have obviously gone through the school system and emerged as happy, healthy, successful members of society. Being an involved and mindful parent, facilitating both intellectual and social/emotional growth in your kids, is what will make the most difference, whatever style of schooling or homeschooling you choose.

> **TIP:** There are lots of benefits to homeschooling, and different families will value different benefits. Be involved and engaged with your child, have fun together, do your best, and relax. If things aren't working, try something different.

Homeschooling Benefits: Children Less Preoccupied with Peer Acceptance

Summary of the article by William R. Mattox Jr., San Francisco Chronicle, Friday, March 19, 1999

Although many people imagine homeschooled children to be both socially isolated and socially awkward, research by Brian Ray of the National Home Education Research Institute shows that for most homeschooled families the reality is quite different. Ray reports that typical homeschooled kids participate in 5.2 social activities outside the home each week. These activities include both programs with conventionally schooled kids and field trips or programs with other homeschooled kids. They include things like dance classes, Scout troops, sports teams, church groups, and theater groups, as well as neighborhood play.

One big distinguishing feature, though, is that homeschooled kids generally interact with more people of different ages than conventionally schooled kids do. This is, in fact, more like the "real world" than most people realize—what business environment is composed solely of people born in the same year? This age diversity helps home-schooled kids avoid some of the comparisons made between kids their age, which helps homeschooled "late bloomers" avoid the stigma of being labeled behind or slow. This is just one of the reasons homes-choolers average 30-37 percentile points higher on the most common K-8 standardized tests than conventionally schooled students.

Another difference is that homeschooled kids usually identify themselves with their families rather than with school kids who feel isolated from the adult world and alienated from their parents. Author Patricia Hersch followed conventionally schooled kids through adolescence, titling her book *A Tribe Apart* to describe how those teens felt isolated from the rest of life. Author and public high school teacher David Guterson makes the same case in *Family Matters: Why Homeschooling Makes Sense* (Harcourt-Brace Jovanovich, 1992). He says that the kids he teaches are preoccupied with peer acceptance and commercial culture, and that the social aspects of school encourage a sense of alienation from people of other ages.

Susannah Sheffer, author of *A Sense of Self* (Heinemann, 1997) and editor of the *Growing Without Schooling* newsletter from 1986 to 1999, studied self-esteem among adolescent girls. She found that homes-chooled girls didn't lose confidence in themselves the way conventionally schooled girls did when their opinions and ideas diverged from those of their peers. They were more able to hold unique opinions and still hold on to both their friendships and their identities.

This doesn't mean that every homeschooler is socially well-adjusted or that homeschooling is the only way to raise children well. It doesn't mean that conventional schools are terrible. These studies do suggest, though, that homeschooling offers more than just educational benefits, which is why more people are giving it a try.

A brief history of education and homeschooling

"Study the past if you would define the future."

– CONFUCIUS

Education has evolved over time. If we look back far enough, to tribal times, and even in some rare tribes today, learning was a group effort. Children learned useful life skills through play and imitation, and were free to learn about what interested them. They learned from their parents, from older children, and from all the other people in their tribe. As settlements formed, apprenticeships, whether formal or informal, became an important way to learn. Literacy was the province of a very tiny portion of the population when every document was handwritten. For a while in Europe the Catholic Church was the only place one could learn to read and write, and even then only in Latin. The printing press changed all that, and learning to read became more common. Small schools sprang up over time, but the majority of people learned at home or from literate neighbors. A few of those learned with the help of tutors and governesses, but for most that was not the case. In the United States, schools became more prevalent, and it was generally considered a privilege to be able to attend rather than a necessity. Compulsory schooling for boys had begun in what was then Prussia, for the purpose of building a strong military.

In the United States it was the Industrial Revolution that led to compulsory schooling. The tycoons of the day needed workers—and lots of them—for their factories. What they needed were people who knew just enough to be highly productive, but who had been trained to not question authority, to accept their lot in life, and to have their days regulated by starting bells, lunch bells, and ending bells. The businessmen pushed hard for compulsory schooling based on the Prussian model, which would train future factory workers and keep any young upstarts too busy to form their own competing businesses.

They claimed it was for the common good, but they certainly never sent their own children to public school. For a more thorough look at the beginnings of compulsory schooling, read John Taylor Gatto's *The Underground History of American Education*. Unfortunately, although our technology and need for knowledge has changed dramatically since the Industrial Revolution, our school system has not.

One of the first and certainly most vocal proponents of homeschooling was John Holt. He started as a schoolteacher in private schools, hoping that the private school structure would be more conducive to learning than public school. It wasn't. He spent years observing children and how they learned, and in the 1960s he wrote *How Children Learn* and *How Children Fail*. Finally, after giving up on reforming the school system, he wrote *Instead of Education*, which recommended removing children completely from school and giving them more rights. It was a radical departure from the whole idea of school, not just schooling at home, but unschooling, giving children control over their own learning. Enough parents were interested in this that he started a newsletter for homeschooling parents: *Growing Without Schooling*.

In the beginning, there were very small numbers of people who homeschooled, and those who did often had to band together to fight for their rights to do so. It was a small, inclusive community, even if the main ways they encouraged one another was through letters, phone calls, the newsletters written by John Holt and by the Moore family, and the Hegeners' *Home Education Magazine*. They homeschooled *to* homeschool, for the sake of the children. It was an ethos, a way of life, and they were all in it together. Holt's final book, *Teach Your Own*, with Pat Farenga, is worth reading, as is his *Learning All the Time*.

In the mid 1980s several national organizations were launched by conservative Christians that changed the public face of homeschooling considerably. Instead of inclusivity, these groups focused on becoming exclusive, severing contact with homeschool groups who remained welcoming to all, and dropping all mention of them from their newsletters, including paid advertisements. It's easier to find these religious groups, as they have plenty of venues for marketing and cross-promoting one another, and they are usually the ones in the news. It can be a lot harder to find secular groups. They're out there, but they don't have the platform to promote themselves in the same way. A good article on the history of this is "Who Stole Homeschooling?" by Cheryl Lindsey Seelhoff, on the hsislegal.com website.

Homeschooling is changing yet again. It is no longer a tiny movement of radical parents, nor of people who have completely given up on our educational system. It never was a solely religious movement. Now it seems everybody I speak to knows at least one family that homeschools or has done so in the past. And no longer is homeschooling only for those who have chosen to homeschool the whole family. Over the last ten years more and more families have joined the homeschool community who are homeschooling to meet the needs of a particular child. It has become less about bucking the system or religious instruction and more about providing individual attention.

When we first moved to Minnesota and joined some homeschool groups, everyone else either had homeschooled right from the beginning or had taken their children out early and were dedicated to homeschooling all their kids. As time has gone by, we are seeing parents pulling individual children out of school and homeschooling one or two while the others remain in conventional school. It's an interesting trend to watch, and it has helped to change my mindset about the kinds of things successful homeschooling can be. It is so individual! I see people who, after homeschooling, send one or more of their kids to junior high or high school and love it, whereas others are removing their children after the system has failed them. There is no one right way to educate people.

TIP: While homeschooling may seem like a very unconventional way to raise children, if we look at history, it's compulsory schooling that is the anomaly. It's an experiment in social control that has become entrenched in our society.

Is homeschooling legal?

"I have never let my schooling interfere with my education."
– ATTRIBUTED TO MARK TWAIN

Yes, homeschooling is legal in all 50 U.S. states and many other countries. And no, you do not need to retain a lawyer to be able to homeschool. Homeschooling is growing more popular, and the most recent U.S. Department of Education statistics show the number of homeschooled students doubled from 1999 to 2012, to an estimated 1.8 million students, or 3.4% of all school age-children (U.S. Department of Education, National Center for Education Statistics, Homeschooling in the United States: 2012-(NCES 2016096)).

Homeschooling requirements differ by state, so find a homeschool organization in your state that can help you cover all your bases. Also check out the A-to-Z Homeschooling website listed in the resources section. Some states implement more oversight than others and will request that you show how you are covering each subject. Our family tends toward unschooling and away from the stereotypical idea of sitting in desks following a curriculum as much as possible, although that style does work for some families. The various styles are summarized in chapter two.

In complying with state requirements, you may have to be creative in how you label learning experiences to get past school-at-home type forms. For example, some states require that you list the days of your school year. In our house, every day is a day of learning, so we are a year-round school. In fact, our summers are sometimes busier than the rest of the year, especially with physical education and extracurricular activities, field trips (and road trips), and hands-on learning.

For us, Minnesota has been a wonderful place to homeschool. The requirements include filing an annual form with your school superintendent and an immunization or exemption form at specified intervals, and testing your children annually using an officially recog-

nized test. Accepted tests range from standard bubble tests administered by parents to oral tests administered by an official tester to
online tests. Minnesota has a list of subjects that ought to be covered,
which can be overwhelming, and I don't think they are necessarily
covered in any depth in public school. We generally end up covering
most of them without specifically trying, in our explorations of the
world. I first started off with books like *What Your Kindergartener
Needs to Know*. Those quickly fell by the wayside as I discovered that
such books work best if you consider your kids to be quiet, obedient
learning machines. Not ours!

In some states, you might need to list subjects covered and file
it with your school district or state. No need to stress out about
any of it. There are plenty of ways to cover what they need to know
without reading from a list of requirements and trying to cram it all
into a curriculum. While they are young you can cover nutrition and
measurements and fractions while cooking together, health and safety
at the park and the doctor's office, and more math during allowance
time and while getting change at the store. And through reading, not
to mention using the computer. There are so many fun and educational books and computer programs and videos out now that engage
a child's interest much more thoroughly than textbooks. My oldest
now has his own checkbook, and we transfer money into his account
to pay for things like music lessons. Then he writes a check and bal-
ances his checkbook. It's the best kind of learning: life learning. Once
you start looking, you will notice opportunities like this all around
you. Every family is different, and the needs of each child are different. The beauty of homeschooling is that you can tailor the learning
approach for each child and what works best at the time. Then you
can figure out how what you are learning can fit into the categories
that are required, rather than the other way around.

There are other states that are much more restrictive and have
specific curriculum requirements. If you and your kids are thriving
working at grade level and checking in daily, more power to you. If
it's too rigid and stressful and you're wondering why people keep

saying homeschooling is fun, it's because it's school-at-home, which leads to burnout in many homeschooling families. Educate yourself on the various requirements of your state to see if there is a way to work around them in order to make homeschooling better fit your family. Also look at the requirements of other states; you might consider moving, or you might work with other homeschoolers to change your legislation using the precedent of other states' laws.

TOM SAYS: At the very best, the laws written by politicians will be from the point of view of traditional education, with little understanding of how learning works in non-school environments. At worst, these laws will be written by people who are opponents of homeschooling and are attempting to discourage it.

One thing to watch out for are school administrators who are not familiar with state laws on homeschooling. Many school districts promote their own "requirements" above and beyond what you are legally required to provide. I know a number of people who were asked to fill out all kinds of unnecessary paperwork by their school districts, and I have even heard of schools threatening to call truant officers on parents who wish to remove their children from school. If you know what the law is and can quote it to them, they will have no basis to stand on. Furthermore, you might just educate them, and in the process make it easier for the next family who would like to homeschool.

Another good idea is to check with different homeschool organizations, because you might get different advice from different sources. We use the form provided by the Minnesota Homeschoolers' Alliance (MHA), which is short and sweet and covers everything required by law. It's reassuring to know that the form provided by the Minnesota Association of Christian Home Educators (MACHE) is quite similar, but that's not always the case. Some homeschool groups feel that supplying more information is better, so check around. Sometimes the legislators themselves aren't exactly clear on how to apply the laws they have enacted; MHA regularly contacts our state liaison to clarify what homeschoolers should do when the wording of the law is ambiguous. Presumably most of the other local groups either do something similar or use the most updated info from larger groups.

There are two schools of thought about giving more information than the legal minimum. One holds that providing the state or district with as much information as possible will circumvent any future questions or legal problems, whereas the other holds that if everyone provides more information than is legally required it will eventually become a requirement. This would increase the burden for future homeschoolers, making homeschooling more onerous and less accessible. Also consider that you might yourself be asked in the future to provide extra information if you start out that way. We opt for the "less is more" mindset, which is less stressful for us, as well as less time-consuming.

TIP: Find a homeschooling organization in your state to ask about legal requirements. Other homeschoolers can help you navigate the system and give you the information you need to exercise your right to homeschool.

Can I really teach my own kids?

"It does not matter how slowly you go as long as you do not stop."
– CONFUCIUS

Absolutely you can teach your kids yourself! So many people have said to me, "I wish I could do that!" Well, you can. Yes, there are hurdles such as job schedules and single parenting which I will address later. The biggest worry people have is that they don't have experience as a schoolteacher, and may not have done particularly well in school. So what if you're not a teacher? You are a capable person who loves your kids. You probably made it through school, and even if you didn't you know how to navigate in your world. If you wanted to find out about baking pastries or woodworking or raising hedgehogs or nuclear physics, you could ask a friend or read a book or watch a You-Tube video or take a class. The same goes for learning with your kids. I've learned a lot myself as we've followed their interests (and mine). It might even be harder for you if you are a teacher, as there will be more to unlearn about what works in homeschooling. Really watch your children as they are discovering something new, be present to the joy and excitement of true learning. Notice how you are most and least helpful in the process, and you will see that traditional teaching styles can actually get in the way of learning. In fact, I often find that any intervention I make as an educator rather than a suggestion as a collaborator gets in the way of learning.

When my kids were younger, I learned all kinds of new things like the different types of construction vehicles, how many drive wheels various steam locomotives had, and the sizes of carnivorous dinosaurs that lived in the Jurassic period. Now we're exploring geology, Norse mythology, and global warming. Did I learn all that in school? Nope. We touched on some of it, like geology and dinosaurs, and now I am having a great time learning more along with my kids.

Many people are hesitant to jump into homeschooling because they don't feel they have the tools they need to provide the best education for their children. Schools are not set up to cater to the individual needs of any given child, and no matter how caring a teacher is, he or she cannot spend significant time with any one student. You can. And you can spend as much time on any particular subject as your child needs. You can even delay a subject if your child isn't ready for it yet and come back to it another time and, if necessary, with a different approach.

What if it's a subject you're not any good at? Don't worry, there are plenty of resources out there to help you along the way. Feel like you can't do math and don't want to slog your way through a curriculum? There are multiple online programs to choose from that teach math. Although some of them simply instruct, others come with homework assignments and quizzes and issue certificates at the end. Some libraries offer free homework help. Or you could join a co-op and find a really good math instructor, which is what we did starting with sixth grade. (Yes, my husband is awesome at math, and I'm not so bad myself. However, our oldest sat in on a math class at the co-op, absolutely loved the instructor, and has been taking classes from her ever since.) You could even hire a high school or college student to tutor your kids. And finally, consider this: What if your job ultimately isn't to impart a bunch of concrete knowledge to your kids? What if it's to help them find their own way, and then help them find the resources they need to learn those things?

Sure, we might miss a few things along the way. Here's the thing: Did you learn everything you needed to learn in K-12? Or even college? Learning should never stop, and anything that interests you can be learned at any age. There will always be gaps, whether at home or at school. At least at home your family can choose what to focus on, and you can have your kids growing up knowing that they can always seek out knowledge to fill those gaps on their own initiative and at their own pace. Every teacher is a person like you, and every curriculum is written by a person like you. Those people decided on a goal and spent time learning what they needed to learn to become teachers and curriculum writers. You only need to learn how your own children learn, and show them how to explore the world with you. Your job is much easier, and much more personal.

Reading

A friend of mine, Dori, wrote this about helping her conventionally schooled girls learn to read. She ignored the school's edict about what should happen at home and instead brought mindfulness and joy to the concept of reading:

"I never had my kids read twenty minutes a night, although I did read complicated way-above-their-reading-level books TO them every night; I focused on developing literature lovers rather than "readers" ... which is a fancy way of saying I read to them what *I* liked because it was fun to share my childhood favorites with them.

"For all three of them I spent most of Kindergarten and first grade wondering if they *could* read — I mean, I'd dutifully get out some of the BOB books and painfully work through one or two with them, or I'd convince a kid to stumble through one of those dreadfully boring "I Can Read! Level 1" books with me—and it was miserable for both of us—and we'd just drop it and move on to more fun things.

"And then for each of them BOOM! Somewhere in either late first or early second grade, each kid found THE BOOK, the complicated 100+ page chapter book that grabbed their imagination and wouldn't let go, and they didn't put it down until it was done."

 TIP: Believe in yourself! You and your children can succeed, and you will find all the resources you need if you just keep moving forward and doing the best you can every day.

There's so much out there...
Where do I start?

"Play is the work of childhood."

– FRED ROGERS

First, start by deciding that you're going to homeschool. Everything else flows from that resolve. If you are sure in your mind it is what you want to do, it will be much easier to go forward. Then with that commitment—and your reasons for it—get the rest of the family on board. Remember that you can always change your mind or adjust your approach to doing things; it isn't set in stone. Just be clear that homeschooling is what you think is best right now.

Look up the relevant laws, file your forms, and take your kids out of school. In Minnesota, if your child has never attended school, then you do not need to file any forms until the fall after your child turns seven. If they've attended preschool or any other program that would put them on the books in the school system, then you generally do need to file your forms to let them know that you are homeschooling, even if they are younger than seven, although there are some loopholes for avoiding that. If you are unclear about the laws in your state, find a local group to ask. Parents on our local Facebook pages are perpetually asking for clarification on the "not until age seven" question, because the wording of the law is ambiguous and varies from state to state.

Reasons People Homeschool

The U.S. Department of Education says that the top self-reported reasons for homeschooling (listed as important or most important) in 2012 were:

A concern about environment of other schools 91%
A desire to provide moral instruction 77%
A dissatisfaction with academic instruction at other schools 74%

A desire to provide religious instruction 64%

A desire to provide a nontraditional approach to child's education ... 44%

Other reasons 37%

Child has other special needs 16%

Child has a physical or mental health problem 15%

U.S. Department of Education, National Center for Education Statistics, Homeschooling in the United States: 2012-(NCES 2016096).

If you've never sent your kids to traditional school because you're just getting started on this educational journey, some of this next advice won't apply to your family.

Once you take your kids out of school, your first task is to deschool both them and yourself. What the heck is deschooling? It's decompressing from school, except longer. If you want your kids to take charge of their own learning, to be motivated and have fun, they need a giant break from the stress of school and having their education fed to them. How giant? It depends. It depends on your kids and how excited they are about learning, and it depends on how long they've been in school. A typical recommendation from veteran homeschoolers is up to one month of deschooling for every year of traditional school attended, and it seems like a good rule of thumb. Use your own judgment as to what feels right as your family goes through the process. Your state's laws may require you to report what they are learning, or that you are following a particular curriculum. If you feel that not getting enough deschooling will be detrimental to your child's mental and educational health, you may need to be creative in the ways that you fulfill the state's requirements.

If you're taking your kids out of school because the educational system is stressing them out and sucking the joy out of learning, you will need to do something completely different for a while. Take a vacation if you can swing it. Hey, you're homeschooling now—you can go places in the off season and miss all the crowds!

Talk to your kids about the process before deschooling them, and keep an eye out for how they are responding. Some kids will love the idea and embrace it wholeheartedly, whereas others might need longer to get past the feeling that they need to be told what to do with their time. You might want to start out with lots of fun activities and gradually taper off the number of scheduled items as they become used to having more autonomy. It's possible they will not know what to do with free time at first, since they may not have had very much of it recently. They might even complain of being bored, because they are not used to coming up with their own ideas and activities. I currently counter complaints of boredom in our house by reminding them that being bored is a perfect opportunity for their brains to come up with something creative and interesting. Even though we rarely have to field that complaint, it usually occurs after school friends have come to play. (It also happens as teenage hormones start to hit the brain in boys, as discussed in Louann Brizendine's *The Male Brain*.)

As you plan fun activities and outings, let your kids help choose where to go and how long to stay. Help them build up their sense of autonomy and agency. Remember that they may resist homeschooling because they are missing their friends. Make sure to schedule time for them to see their old friends, and attend homeschooling groups where they can meet a variety of new people.

You need this down time, too. I suspect that, as parents, you have been fighting with the system (and possibly even your kids) while trying to get the best for them. Revel in the fact that you no longer have to harangue your kids about homework, help organize fundraisers for school equipment, or argue on the phone with administrators. Relax and have some fun instead. Be present to the gift of having time together just being. It will most likely be a change from the constant demands of being busy accomplishing something. Spend time as a family rebuilding those bonds that have been stressed. Remember that learning a subject happens quickly when the brain is relaxed and engaged, and slowly or not at all when it is under stress. That means there is plenty of time to chill out before diving into academic subjects.

As a parent, you may also find you need to do some deschooling yourself, not just to relax but to uncouple your ideas about education from your ideas about school. Do you feel that having fun can't be educational? Or that learning has to be hard work? Neither of those things is true. Watch your kids while they play and relax, and see what they learn. See how quickly or slowly they learn, and how joyfully they learn when it's self-directed. Then compare that to what learning is like in school, and see if that helps you to gain some insight and confidence into the homeschooling process.

While practicing being present with your kids, spend some time together shaping your home into a learning environment. You may want to set up a family space for learning and projects of all kinds, and consolidate interesting books and materials. On the other hand, you may want to spread everything out so that each room has plenty to do. Make sure you get your kids involved in the process, so they can take ownership of their environment as well as their education. My kids have come up with some great ideas about ways to organize the house so that we can fit everything into our rather small space. For example, when we got a larger couch and had to remove a bookcase to fit it in, the boys brainstormed with me to figure out where to put the bookcase instead.

Here are some suggestions for things to do while deschooling. Please don't try to do all of them at once! The whole point is to relax and explore your interests. Pick a few to enjoy, and leave room for plenty of downtime.

- Sample local and online homeschool groups to find some that suit your family
- Connect with friends, relatives, and other people important to you
- Get out of town, visit the grandparents, or travel somewhere new
- Take yoga or other exercise classes
- Have outings to the library
- Read for fun - on the couch, in hammocks, at the park, or on the beach
- Go to museums, historic sites, and galleries

- Go to concerts, plays, music in the park, or have a dance party
- Go to movies, or have movie marathons at home
- Play a bunch of video games (preferably together)
- Listen to audiobooks together
- Go to lots of parks
- Go camping as a family
- Take a staycation and go see all those tourist places around town that you've been missing
- Work on life skills such as cooking, woodworking, or bike repair
- Make stuff together - Legos, origami, knitting, artwork, photo albums, pottery... anything!
- Work together on projects such as gardening, building a fort, or redecorating a room
- Go hiking or biking or take walks together around the neighborhood
- Join Scouts or Campfire or 4H or another outdoor group
- Join or form a book club
- Join a theater group

The purpose of deschooling is to let the mind relax and become open to learning again, and to help us understand that learning and school aren't the same thing. On a lazy day when you have good rapport with your kids, ask them about what kinds of things they would like to learn and do. You can brainstorm together and suggest things if it feels right. Just make sure that you find out what they want to learn about and how they would like to learn it. Use that as your starting point for homeschooling. It might not look much like traditional education. It might look like programming video games or making historical costumes or visiting a farm. Or it might look like reading non-fiction books and watching documentaries. It might even look like workbooks and school. Just make the experiences as rich, interesting, and fun as you can. Remember that there is no rush. People learn things very quickly when they are interested in them, much faster than in school. Learning only takes 12 years of long days when administered by traditional schools.

If your kids are young and haven't been to school yet, congratulations! You don't need to deschool them unless you have been pressuring them to achieve at a young age. You've probably already been doing a bunch of fun stuff that's on the list, and you may have noticed something interesting. Most of those things on the list are considered educational for the young brain. You've already been educating your children, and there's no reason to stop doing just that. There is no magic switch in the brain that makes sitting at a desk something to look forward to the second they hit "school age." Different children are ready to do more serious work at different ages, some of which runs along gender lines. For a deeper look into early-education gender differences, read chapter two of *Raising Cain* by Dan Kindlon and Michael Thompson. As your kids mature and are ready for it, slowly add in the more academic subjects.

Our youngest is teaching himself how to write because he wants to make tickets and handbills for magic-show performances. He's been playing with his brothers' magic trick gadgets and watching videos of magicians, and his interest in writing has sprung out of that. He is using stencils, a set of rubber alphabet stamps, and plain writing to make his mark, and in his mind it's all play. Or perhaps everything he does is work to him. But it's self-imposed work and therefore meaningful and engaging.

What is Deschooling?
HomeschoolGroupHug.com

For Grownups: What is Deschooling?
As adults, we need to put ideas like those below out of our heads:

- The school environment and methods provide the best possible education
- Children's learning happens on a schedule
- Learning only happens through teaching
- Kids are best kept in same-age packs

- Repetition, worksheets, and rote learning are the way to go
- Kids cannot socially interact outside their age range

I'm sure you can think of many other ideas and thought processes that need to be deschooled out of the typical grown-up product of the education system. It's not uncommon for close friends and family to require some deschooling before they can get behind your new educational model, too. That can be a challenge to engineer!

For Kids: What is Deschooling?

Deschooling here refers to the mental changes a student goes through after removal from school or another institute of learning. The school mindset must be "deprogrammed" over time and the child must adapt to a new environment having far less regulation and structure. It is a period of adjustment.

Some kids may pine for school mates, some may find they can't occupy their time without being told what to do, others may be concerned about being identified as homeschoolers and attending homeschool events.

It will come with time; the longer they've been in school, the longer this process can take.

TIP: Take time off before jumping in to homeschooling. Remember to play together as a family and with friends. Learning and living should be fun, for you as well as for your kids.

How do I keep my kids from being hermits?

"Wherever it is you may be, it is your friends who make your world."

– **CHRIS BRADFORD,** *YOUNG SAMURAI: THE WAY OF THE SWORD*

The socialization question has become a running joke with homeschoolers, since all we seem to hear is, "But what about socialization?" There is an entire book with this title that is a review of scientific studies on socialization and homeschooling. Everybody asks this question of homeschoolers, who get very tired of it. It seems to be the biggest objection non-homeschoolers have and one of the biggest reasons *to* homeschool for those who do.

The short answer to the socialization question is to get out of the house and hang out with friends. Homeschooled kids are generally quite well socialized without going to school. Very few people spend all day every day in the house studying, and socialization is really not a problem for most homeschoolers. Yes, there are occasional people you hear about who keep their kids locked away. That's called abuse, not homeschooling, and if you're worried about your kids being hermits it's very likely you aren't that kind of person.

I like to ask a different question: "What do you mean by socialization?" If by socialization you mean kids are socialized to be exactly like other school kids and generally only interact with kids in their grade, forming cliques and pressuring each other to not stand out from the crowd, or conform with the nonconformists, then no, homeschooling won't do that. In fact, some psychologists suggest that the popular idea of socialization with peers is actually peer dependence when not balanced with enough healthy relationships with adults as mentors.

If by socialization you mean instead that kids grow up to be happy, well-adjusted, contributing members of society who are comfortable interacting with a large range of people of various backgrounds and ages, then yes, absolutely, homeschooling is a great way to do that. If you need to have facts and figures and studies to convince family members that you won't be ruining your children, grab yourself a copy of one of the books on homeschoolers' social life. An excellent and comprehensive one is *The Well-Adjusted Child* by Rachel Gathercole.

For evidence of homeschooler social skills, let's look at one of our annual homeschool events, the Imagination Fair. It's like a science fair except the projects can be about anything from science to art to history. One year the fair happened to coincide with my mother's visit, and I talked her into being a judge. As a biology professor, she is often asked to judge science fairs. When I first spoke with her about our intention to homeschool she was pretty concerned about the socialization aspect. Since then she has come to appreciate that homeschooling, far from stunting our kids, is enriching their lives in ways none of us had expected. The Imagination Fair was a good opportunity for her to interact one-on-one with thirty or so homeschooled students other than her grandsons and talk about the projects and ideas that interest them. After the fair she told me how impressed she was by the students. She said they were all very articulate and engaged with their projects, and they didn't hesitate to make eye contact while speaking with her. They were easier to talk to and seemed to find it easier to talk to her than the usual science fair students. They also were more confident in themselves and their work. That sounds like pretty decent socialization to me.

What most people consider to be good socialization—rather than conformity, peer pressure, and bullying—often takes place during extracurricular time anyway. School teaches you to sit down, be quiet, and shun collaborating with other kids unless that's part of the curriculum. You may socialize at recess (which is phased out by sixth or seventh grade) and lunch, and generally only with students in your same grade. You learn how to compete with one another, and how to judge yourself and others by the ability to regurgitate knowledge on a test, as well as by superficial measures such as physical beauty and clothing styles. What kind of socialization is that? The teacher-to-student ratio leaves much to be desired, and teachers have less time and fewer resources than they once did. And while bullying is frowned upon, it still happens on a regular basis in schools, where it may or may not be dealt with sufficiently. Who is helping students learn good models of interaction? Parents, friends' parents, coaches, Scout leaders, spiritual leaders, and other mentors outside of school, in addition to a few exceptional school teachers. That's who. If the most desirable kinds of socialization are taking place primarily at home and in the community rather than in school, the whole argument for school as a place to learn good behavior falls short.

"If schools were necessary for healthy social development, then nearly the whole of mankind would have been utterly unable to function interpersonally until the advent of compulsory schooling just two hundred years ago. And yet the human race has successfully carried on, co-existed, and grown since its inception, bringing us right up to modern times. Members of the earlier human race were socialized in the real world - that is, in families and communities..." *The Well-Adjusted Child*, page 40. In much of Africa today, the whole village is still involved in raising a child.

"Language, socializing, and the human brain co-evolved with each other, allowing us to excel over many of the physical and mental skills of other mammals and primates." - paraphrased by Mark Waldman, author of *How God Can Change Your Brain*, Ballantine Books (March 23, 2010); research originally from *The Symbolic Species: The Co-Evolution of Language and the Brain*, Deacon, T., Norton (April 17, 1998).

Although going to school may seem like a perfectly normal way to grow up to those of us who did it, in fact the isolation and segregation of school kids from the community and one another is not the historical norm. It is, instead, a strange way to teach kids how to function well in the community.

One incorrect assumption people make is that spending time with parents means not spending time with friends. In the school system structure, it is often the case that friends and parents are mutually exclusive. Your friends are at school and your parents are at home, and your parents don't want your friends around during the "quality time" they have to squeeze in at dinnertime and on the weekends. This can also add to the antagonism of children, especially teenagers, toward parents, as they have to choose between friends and family. Dr. William Sears describes what happens as the "detachment snowball" in *The Baby Book*. The more time parents and kids spend apart, the less parents know and understand their kids, and vice versa. Over time they become less responsive, communicative, and respectful toward each other, and thus need more time apart from each other, and the whole thing snowballs. Dr. Sears refers to young children, but the idea holds true throughout life. Homeschoolers have plenty of quality time with their parents and plenty of quality time with their friends. Students are not segregated from their parents for eight hours a day, nor are they separated from their friends when they are around their parents. They can have the best of both worlds, and with a little help from their parents they can avoid some of the worst problems found in the school setting. Beyond that, parents can gain confidence in their parenting skills by spending so much more time with their children.

Homeschoolers actually have a number of advantages in the socialization department. They have role models in their parents, their friends' parents, and other adults, and they generally have friends of all ages who can help them learn skills, patience, and flexibility. During educational time they can ask as many questions as necessary to learn course material (and life skills), and the teacher-to-student ratio is excellent. They often work together with siblings or other students of a variety of ages who are interested in learning the same things. Squirmy kids can take frequent recess breaks, and there is no need for busywork while waiting for the rest of the class to finish. They learn to value others' skills that are different than their own, assuming that their learning environment values those skills.

Because learning things doesn't take nearly so long when it isn't institutionalized, homeschoolers have a lot more time for those extracurricular activities like music, sports, theater, field trips, and just hanging out with friends. Because parents are usually along, they are available to model good interactions and step in to mediate when necessary. This teaches valuable life skills and doesn't throw the kids into situations that they don't yet know how to navigate alone. On the other hand, having parents along doesn't automatically mean helicopter parenting. The parents are often busy socializing among themselves or getting some work done while keeping an eye out for anything that requires intervention as the children play. If a situation occurs in which something needs to be changed, the structure of homeschool groups generally lends itself to discussion of the problem and fixing it. If that doesn't resolve the issue, homeschoolers are free to leave a situation in which bullying is occurring, any situation in which the social or learning aspects are less than desired, or even a group that just isn't clicking for them.

But What About Socialization?

Snappy answers to the socialization question from homeschooling parents:

"We prefer to bully him and steal his lunch money at home."

"Didn't your teacher tell you that you're *not* there to socialize in class?"

"I've seen the village, and I don't want it socializing my children."

"We want our kids civilized, not socialized."

"You don't go to school anymore, how do *you* manage to socialize?"

"Well, I guess I can teach them how to swear, pretend they don't know the answers, and wait in line to use the bathroom, but why?"

"Do you mean socialization or socializing?"

"I socialize my dog, I educate my children."

"I prefer to socialize my children in a small, loving environment, the same way I prefer to educate them."

"Socialization? That IS why I homeschool."

"Socialization can be such a problem. I have to limit them or we'd never get any work done."

Full disclosure: My family was the problem family in one of the groups we belonged to. While my oldest was never mean-spirited, he has some sensory processing issues and needs more physical stimulation than most people. He has lots of energy and needs to move. A lot. He sits on a yoga ball and bounces when we watch movies at home, although he's matured enough to be able to sit still at a theater. He has always enjoyed things like roller coasters, deep tissue massage, and rowdy play. Unfortunately, when he was younger and had less control, it also meant that other kids around him often got hurt. He lacks the sensory feedback to tell him when something is too much, so he had to learn it intellectually. At the time, I had no idea that there was occupational therapy that could help him, and we ended up being asked to leave the group. Now people look at me with disbelief when I tell them this story, because they can't imagine him being a problem.

I suspect that if he had been in school, we might have spent years searching for a school that wouldn't kick him out—and he would have gotten a reputation as a troublemaker (and one who couldn't read, to boot, as he wasn't ready to do any serious reading until age 11). But being that we are homeschoolers, it didn't derail the educational process for us. We just kept learning as usual. It did lead us to examine how we could better support our son in being successful in social interactions, and we found that smaller groups and more structured play (like board games and organized sports) work much better for him than larger, more unstructured groups. Finding a school with classrooms of three to ten students can be a tall order. Fortunately as homeschoolers we had a lot of flexibility when it came to both educational groups and social groups, and we found co-op classes and social settings that fit our needs.

What about diversity? If exposing your children to diverse races, cultures, and ideas is important to you, then it is likely that you will foster those experiences whether or not your children are in school. They may not encounter the sheer number of people they would meet in a school, but at the same time the circumstances in which they meet people may well foster greater understanding and lasting friendships. It is true that the homeschool community in general is not currently very diverse, although that is changing, albeit slowly. You can counteract that lack of diversity. Take your kids out into the community, volunteer with them, go to ethnic restaurants and meet the proprietors, welcome diversity into your homeschool groups, make an effort. Your attitude will make all the difference.

Obviously not all homeschoolers are socialized the same way, and it's a good thing, too. If your family members are all introverts who prefer online classes, then you are likely to have to go out of your way to meet other people, and you'll have to build that into your curriculum. If your family members are all extroverts who would prefer to spend their time in groups doing extracurricular activities, then you will need to focus on making sure the academic subjects are covered. Our family has both introverts and extroverts, and we can tailor our days to meet our needs—including the parents' needs—for both interaction and downtime. That's right. Make sure to take care of yourself as well as your kids. As a bonus, we can have sick days or mental health days when we need them, without having to worry about attendance or doctors' notes. It's not very frequent, but it's always nice to know that we can cancel our plans for the day without lasting repercussions.

On a related note, I'd like to mention something about introversion. In the current American culture, extroverts are more valued than introverts, whereas the opposite is true in places like Japan. I recommend the book *Quiet* by Susan Cain for anyone with an introvert in the family. There is even a version for kids. It was very helpful for our introverted son to better understand himself and feel more valued. It has been a major benefit to our family to tailor our social events to our children, rather than trying to make them all fit into the extrovert mold. I think they all have better self-esteem than they otherwise would have had. They are certainly much more confident about themselves and their abilities than my husband and I were at their age.

"If someone argued that a prison inmate was getting better preparation for the outside world by being in prison (and surrounded mostly by other inmates) than an ordinary citizen could get by living in the outside world, people might understandably think this person was deluded or crazy. Yet the argument is often made that children confined to school every day are in a better position to learn skills for living in the 'real world' than children who are not.

"History has shown, and we shall see for ourselves, that home-schoolers, who are educated in the 'outside' world rather than inside a classroom, function exceptionally well in the 'real world.'" *The Well-Adjusted Child*, p. 168

TIP: The hardest thing about socialization for homeschoolers is convincing your friends and family that you're not ruining your kids. Opportunities are all around you, from neighborhood kids to homeschool groups to volunteering to extracurricular classes to online forums. Make friends and have fun.

Where will I find the patience?

"Children will still look up to us even if we're candid about our limitations, even if we speak to them from our hearts, and even if they can see that...we're still just people struggling to make our way in the world...In fact, the more real we are with them, the more likely it is that they'll feel real respect for us."

– ALFIE KOHN, *UNCONDITIONAL PARENTING*

To have patience with your kids, first you must be kind to yourself. Sometimes that means taking a break from your kids. For most families, that means sending them to school, just like 96.6% of everyone else. People who are dedicated to homeschooling their kids have to find alternate ways to create breaks. This isn't as hard as it may seem, especially now that you have a better idea of what homeschool families actually do all day instead of sitting around the table "doing school." Finding time for yourself and your spouse is discussed more thoroughly in chapter four—take advantage of some of the ideas there to help recharge yourself.

If forcing the kids to do their homework puts everyone on edge, and you are picturing days on end filled with that kind of interaction, you can relax. One of the reasons you want to home-school is to make learning easier, and the best way to do that is to get everyone on board together rather than forcing them to do work they will resist. At dinner recently we were discussing how our oldest is doing with learning Japanese, which he enjoys. Then I turned to our middle son and told him I really wanted him to get back to learning a foreign language. His whole posture slumped, and he glowered at me. I talked just a little bit about the benefit to your brain when you learn another language, and the benefits of knowing the language when you travel. I mentioned that he could choose a country that he would like to visit someday and use that as motivation. He continued to glower at me. Then I told him that if he really wanted to, he could learn Elvish, as devised by J.R.R.

Tolkien and refined by others. He perked right up. I reminded him that it wouldn't have much real-world applicability, but it would still give him the same brain benefits. He's all in to learn a foreign language now. And even though there won't be a lot of people to speak it with, in this internet age we can find them. He wants his brother to learn it, too, so they can speak it together. And once you have the rudiments of one foreign language, it can be easier for the brain to learn another. That is the kind of thing that can turn homeschooling from an exercise in patience into something that is fun for everyone.

TOM SAYS: *Knowing why you want the kids to learn or do something helps in dealing with situations like this. It can help them understand why you think something is important, and give it more attention, but it also helps you be more flexible in the application of the principle. If you're just telling them to learn a foreign language because everyone is doing it and you think they should too, you have much less flexibility in your own thinking and therefore less ability to find a compromise that works.*

Now, think about what it is that sets you off. What kinds of things drive you up the wall, what things are annoying but manageable unless you've had a long day, and what things roll right off your back? It will be different for each person. Pay attention during the day to the kinds of interactions that are the most stressful for you. The key to teaching kids how to manage their own emotions and stress is to learn how to manage them ourselves. Using mindfulness techniques helps with managing these emotions. Mindfulness is being present in the moment, noticing the emotions we are having to the current situation, and choosing purposefully how we will act rather than react. It doesn't mean always being a perfect parent, but it does mean that as soon as we notice stress reactions we take action to deal with them. We can also teach these techniques to our kids, so that the whole family has a better handle on their emotions.

Bringing mindful parenting practices to homeschooling can change the whole dynamic. It can boost your ability to defuse situations and thus have fewer of those stressful times, and it can help you solve problems that at first seem intractable. There are three simple rules to mindful parenting. **First, assess.** Notice your feelings when you are in conflict with your child. Your feelings could be coming from a variety of places, such as embarrassment that your child is having a public melt-down, frustration because your child is resisting something you think is in their best interest, or fear that your child will never grow out of a particular behavior. When you pinpoint the cause of the emotion, it is easier to step back from it and think more rationally. **Next, pause.** You may think the first step is enough of a pause, but check and make sure you will be able to respond to your child without anger, frustration, or any other emotion that gets in the way of acting from a place of love and kindness. **Finally, listen.** Your child's behavior and reasons make sense to them, even if they don't make sense to you. Listening to them, truly wanting to understand what it's like from their point of view, will help you find common ground. Sometimes just being heard is all that's needed, sometimes knowing what the problem is will help you solve it, and sometimes you might agree to disagree. When you can bring compassion to the table, or at the very least leave the negative feelings behind, patience comes more easily and problems are solved more quickly.

To be more patient in general, I find it helps me to get some exercise on a regular basis. When I notice that I'm getting stressed out I can do deep breathing or a short meditation, and remind myself that the kids are doing the best they can with the resources they have. I try to be calm and mindful, helping them work through what they need to learn now, rather than wondering why they haven't learned it yet and being frustrated that we keep covering the same ground. Their developmental stages are not always easy, and I often have to remind myself that defiance in a five-year-old and mood swings in a pre-teen or teen are normal. It also helps to remember that I am doing the best I can, too. Finally, I just put a stop to whatever is robbing me of my patience. Some strategies I use are: send the kids outside, or separate them and send them to different rooms. Put on a favorite movie for them and go outside while they watch it. Take everyone to the park or out for ice cream, or sit on the couch together for cuddles. Pull out a board game or new toy I've been saving and spend a little together time with just one of the kids. What is important is to take a break from the situation that is making everyone frustrated and spend a couple of minutes reconnecting afterwards. Sometimes after facing a difficult situation I tell them I could really use a hug, and that helps us all restart from a better place.

If just the idea of having the kids at home makes you want to lose your temper, but you can see the benefits of homeschooling and would like to give it a go, there are plenty of options. Start with yourself. Consider meditation, anger management, or a parenting class. Whenever I work on myself, my kids seem to become magically better behaved. If you have a serious personality clash with one (or more) of your kids, consider having your spouse be the at-home parent. Or, if there are grandparents nearby, broach the subject with them. Having grandparents or other close relatives overseeing the homework can be a great option for some families. Don't forget to ask your kids, too. They might have some great ideas, and they'll be more willing to participate when they have some say in their education. Also take note of when and where the clashes are the worst. Is it at home or while out, while doing work or playing, when they're tired or hungry, when there's nothing to do, when it's just the family or just with friends? There may be a pattern, and breaking the pattern could prove helpful. Do homework at the library, have friends over for a study session, spend more time playing or talking together, and spend less time together in the most stressful situations.

After working on myself quite a bit I have become a pretty patient and mellow parent, although my personality tends toward mellow anyway. I am certainly not perfect, nor am I always patient, and there are plenty of homeschooling parents who aren't temperamentally patient or mellow. I find an apology goes a long way when I've lost my temper or been thoughtless with my family. We all do the best we can and hope our kids will be patient with us while we figure this whole parenting thing out.

TIP: Take a deep breath, take plenty of you-time, and remind yourself that you and your kids are all doing the best you can with the resources you have. It's about growing and learning, not about being perfect, and that holds true for all of us.

Resources and References

A2ZHomeschooling.com - A huge compilation of homeschooling resources

HomeschoolGroupHug.com - Resources for homeschooling, unschooling, and travel

homeschoolers.org - Minnesota Homeschoolers Alliance site with advice for MN residents

JohnHoltGWS.com - A great resource for both homeschooling and unschooling

NaturalChild.org - A site for respectful parenting and unschooling

NBTSC.org - Not Back to School Camp for homeschooled teens

TheHomeschoolMom.com - Another good compilation of homeschooling resources

The Baby Book, William Sears M.D. and Martha Sears R.N., New York: Little, Brown & Co., 1993

But What About Socialization? Answering the Perpetual Home Schooling Question: A Review of the Literature, Dr. Susan A. McDowell, Philodeus Press (January 2004)

Dumbing Us Down, John Taylor Gatto, New Society Publishers Anniversary Edition (June 13, 2017)

Euler: The Master of Us All, William Dunham, Dolciani Mathematical Expositions (Book 22), American Mathematical Society (January 1, 1999)

Family Matters: Why Homeschooling Makes Sense, David Guterson, Harcourt, 1st Edition (September 1992)

"Homeschooling Benefits: Children less preoccupied with peer acceptance," William R. Mattox Jr., San Francisco Chronicle, March 19, 1999

The Female Brain, Louann Brizendine, Harmony, Reprint Edition (August 7, 2007)

The Male Brain: A Breakthrough Understanding of How Men and Boys Think, Louann Brizendine, Harmony (January 25, 2011)

"How Mindful Parenting Differs From Just Being Mindful," Jill Ceder, ParentCo, parent.com, August 22, 2107

Quiet: The Power of Introverts in a World That Can't Stop Talking, Susan Cain, Broadway Books (January 29, 2013)

Quiet Power: The Secret Strengths of Introverted Kids, Susan Cain, Gregory Mone, Erica Moroz, Puffin Books, Dgs Rep Edition (May 2, 2017)

Raising Cain: Protecting the Emotional Life of Boys, Dan Kindlon & Michael Thompson, Ballantine Books, 1st Edition (April 4, 2000)

Teach Your Own: The John Holt Book of Homeschooling, John Holt & Pat Farenga, Da Capo Press, First Paperback Edition (April 2003)

The Underground History of American Education, John Taylor Gatto, Oxford, Revised Edition (2006)

The Well-Adjusted Child: The Social Benefits of Homeschooling, Rachel Gathercole, Mapletree Publishing Co., 1st Edition (June 8, 2007)

What Your Kindergartener Needs to Know: Preparing Your Child for a Lifetime of Learning, E.D. Hirsch Jr., Bantam, Revised Updated Edition (July 16, 2013)

"Who Stole Homeschooling?," Cheryl Lindsey Seelhoff, Homeschooling is Legal, February 19th, 2012 http://hsislegal.com/who_stole_homeschooling/

Young Samurai: The Way of the Sword, Chris Bradford, Penguin UK, 2nd Edition (July 2, 2009)

Diving In

How do I choose a homeschooling style?

"Intelligence plus character - that is the goal of true education."
– MARTIN LUTHER KING JR.

What kind of parenting philosophy do you have? This will play a big part in deciding what your homeschooling day looks like. As will your kids' attitudes about structure, formal learning, and exploration. Most homeschooling families that I know have over time evolved a fairly eclectic approach, melding pieces of different styles into something that is uniquely theirs. This happens as families become more relaxed about the structure of homeschooling. With hindsight, the early days of trying to reproduce the school environment seem almost laughable. You're not at school, and for good reason, so why try to recreate it? That doesn't mean throwing the baby out with the bathwater, but it does mean taking a hard look at which experiences will serve your family well and which are counterproductive. The kids hate sitting at the table to do workbooks? Do them while cuddling on the couch or sitting outside. They can't sit still for more than 15 minutes? Take more frequent breaks, and incorporate more movement into learning. They have trouble taking in information by reading it? Get some audiobooks and listen to podcasts. Just because schools expect kids to get most of their information from books by fourth grade doesn't mean all kids will read fluently and do their best learning using books—by fourth or any grade. Below are several different styles that homeschoolers use, with links at the end of the chapter for those wanting more information.

A lot of people start out in a **traditional** style, trying something that looks a lot like "school at home," with students sitting quietly at desks or at a table working with textbooks and workbooks. This is the style most often portrayed in the media, but it can be expensive and has the highest burnout rate. There are online programs and curricula that will give you a structure and the confidence that you are at least covering everything that a school would. This works for some families, most of whom find that the material can be covered in much less time than in a traditional school, leaving free time to explore interests and take field trips. On the other hand, it can be confining, in that it limits the freedom to tailor the education to the student's needs and abilities, plus it is a lot of work for the parents to make the kids comply.

A variety of philosophical schools of learning are structured so they don't reproduce the school experience as it is today, using discussion instead of tests. **Classical** homeschooling is based on a style developed in the Middle Ages that focuses on memorization followed by logical discussion and the creation of eloquent and persuasive arguments. **Charlotte Mason** style sees education as a life and a discipline, rather than a learning of skills, and it emphasizes spending time outside in nature, relying on classic literature instead of textbooks and discussion instead of testing. **Thomas Jefferson** style focuses on classic literature, mentors, depth and breadth of knowledge and real world application of it, and inspiring rather than requiring work.

Unit studies is a style that some prefer in which the family focuses on one main subject at a time, say volcanoes. Under that subject, each student can spend time working to his or her ability on a variety of interests. Where to find volcanoes is geography, how the earth's crust moves to produce volcanoes and the kinds of rock formed by them is geology, how plants and animals are affected by lava flow and ash falls is ecology, measuring the height and side slope of a volcano is math, discussing famous volcanoes like Pompeii and Mount Saint Helens and their effects is history, even hiking a lava field if you are near one is physical education, and so forth. Children of different ages can participate to the extent of their interest and competency. One nice way to document homeschooling progress in unit studies is to create a binder or portfolio for each unit, complete with reports and diagrams, photos of field trips and hands-on activities, tickets from museums or events, even magazine collages or crayon drawings from the younger children.

The **Montessori** method is quite structured in the setup of the environment, in which everything is neat and tidy and thought out beforehand for ease of use for the child and for hands-on learning. There are specific areas set up with manipulatives for practical life, sensory work, math, language, culture & geography, music, and art. "Practical life" includes things like cooking and cleaning and everyday life chores in the curriculum. It is more open-ended in allowing the students to pursue whichever learning activity interests them at the moment, and it stresses that there are no mistakes, only learning.

The **Waldorf** method is a style based on the work of Rudolf Steiner, emphasizing educating the whole child (mind, body, and spirit) in age-appropriate ways. Younger grades work more on arts, music, and movement, whereas older students engage in learning without textbooks, and balancing academic subjects with artistic and practical ones.

Maker (or DIY) homeschooling, which is relatively new, is a hands-on, project-based learning style. It is popular among families that value a focus on creativity and ingenuity and that are generally tech-savvy. These homeschoolers focus on bringing ideas and projects to life, and often also focus on entrepreneurship, making use of resources like diy.org and maker or tinker spaces provided by the community.

Unschooling is the least structured style of homeschooling. It focuses on giving children the responsibility and freedom to learn about what interests them. It does not mean ignoring children and hoping that everything will be all right. It may even be more work than some styles, at least for the parents, especially in the beginning. It means being very attentive to facilitating learning on a daily basis rather than picking curricula periodically and then working on it. Unschoolers have the time to become experts in their areas of interest. Unschooling is what we strive for, although we often fall short. One fun way to encourage learning is to put all kinds of interesting things in the daily path of your children and see what they pick up. Bring back library books on various subjects and see who reads them, then check in to see if they want to pursue the subject further. Pull out a puzzle or bring home a feather or stone and help them learn as much or as little about it as their interest calls for. Show them interesting videos and see which ones capture their imagination. The best approach might be to lead by example. We have so many great educational things around the house that sit around mostly unused. Sometimes the boys get an urge to work on something they haven't seen in a while, but I have found the very best way to get them interested in something is to take it out and start working on it myself. Remember that they can always come back to something at another time, and even if now isn't the right time, if you don't force learning they will be more open to it later. Remember, too, that unschoolers may or may not do well on grade level assessments, since those are designed to assess specific skills. The unschoolers we know generally score well, but that won't be true for every child.

Many people eventually fall under a heading that homeschoolers call **Eclectic**, which means they prefer to take pieces of different philosophies or styles and incorporate them into their educational programs. It's a good way to describe a blending of ideas and techniques, which will change as the family and its individuals grow into and out of different needs. Eclectic homeschoolers can pick and choose the textbooks, field trips, classes, and methods that fit their interests and grade levels. They cover what they feel is the most important, rather than what the author of a particular curriculum has chosen.

There are many different ways to educate your children that don't include picking one school and sending your child there all day, or one curriculum and teaching from it exclusively. Some homeschoolers do send their children to local schools for select classes, such as orchestra or math or something that the school provides that really works, and have them at home for the rest of the day. (This depends on your local school system—some allow for this and some don't.) Some homeschoolers take classes online, from places like the Khan Academy, EdX, or Coursera. Some homeschoolers join or form a co-op to cover things that other parents have expertise in and to share teaching duties. Some homeschoolers start in late elementary or middle school and others homeschool the early years and send the kids to middle or high school. Several families I know have chosen a local democratic school for their older children that is closest to their family philosophy of self-directed learning and giving children responsibility for their own education.

In short, there is no one right way to homeschool. There is no "best" philosophy or curriculum. If there were, wouldn't everyone be doing the same thing? The whole point of homeschooling is that one size does not fit all. Your family is different from my family, and your kids are different not only from my kids but from each other. Here is your chance to play, to make learning fun, and to have it work for your individual children.

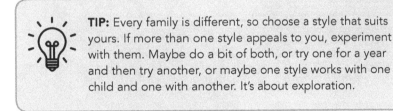

TIP: Every family is different, so choose a style that suits yours. If more than one style appeals to you, experiment with them. Maybe do a bit of both, or try one for a year and then try another, or maybe one style works with one child and one with another. It's about exploration.

Jump Start Your Homeschooling

Kim Jaworski, HomeSchoolResourceSp.com

Here are 25 ideas to help you get excited about homeschooling. These can serve as an interim plan — or they can be the beginning of a whole new approach to learning. There is no "one way" to homeschool. Explore! Create! Make it your own!

1. Take some time and explore your library - or venture to a new library and check it out!

2. Review a "typical course of study" for some ideas and throw them in a hat. Let each child pick a topic from the hat and run with it (research at the library, discover interesting field trips that match

the theme, etc.). Or simply let each child choose a topic that sparks their interest. Older kids can do all the digging for information and then organize it to share with the family (Remember "Show & Tell"?).

3. Pick up a copy of your local tourist information newspaper or brochure or a listing of historical sites and find an adventure that appeals to everyone. Field trips abound!

4. Make a day trip to a neighboring community. Explore their museums, parks, zoos, historical sites, nature centers, etc.

5. Create a survey, then have the kids poll neighbors, relatives, and friends. You might ask, "What is the most interesting thing you ever learned?" or "What is the most amazing thing you have ever seen?" You'll be amazed and delighted at the responses.

6. Pause your formal study and spend time assembling portfolios. It's a great way to review all that you've done and a fun art project, too! (Portfolios for the younger grades can be scrapbook style, displaying brochures of places you have visited or work samplings of art, lessons, etc.).

7. Dig through your game cupboard— Yahtzee, playing cards, Backgammon, chess, dice games, and the like can reinforce strategy skills, logic, math, and more. Play and learn! Discuss strategies for winning or teamwork while playing. (*Hoyle's Rules of Games* can get you started if you want to try a new game or two.)

8. Browse educational supply catalogs and order something new and interesting, or order some different catalogs!

9. Spend some time creating a family newspaper edition—assign reporters to cover family news, interview a relative about a recent event or family history, announce recent births, marriages, etc. Compile it on your computer and share with extended family or friends.

10. Take on a family genealogy project. Document the generations you know, then interview elders, continuing your research online, at the library, or at the historical society. Or create a simple family

timeline (each child could map their own personal timeline as well, from birth to present, listing any events they deem noteworthy). Take it a step further and learn about your family's countries of origin (see #13).

11. Gather up some interesting new recipes from magazines or pull out some family favorites and spend a week cooking and baking.

12. Check out travel videos at your library or through inter-library loan. Take a virtual trip! (This can be a starting point for our next idea. See #13!)

13. Choose a country and make an exploratory study of it—its culture, its customs, its foods, geographic features. Then have some friends over for a special dinner party to showcase what you have learned. (This could be a great New Year's Eve party idea, or the theme for a surprise birthday or anniversary party — "A Trip to [name of country]!")

14. Spend a few days mapping your neighborhood. Maps can be as general or as specific as your kids can handle. Talk about "scale" and "symbols," and use colored pencils or markers to really make it a work of art. Try orienteering.

15. Your library probably has a selection of children's magazines. Spend some time with past issues of *National Geographic World*, Archeology's *DIG*, *Kid's Discover*, or other titles. These issues are packed with interesting tidbits, newsy articles, and fun crafts and activities, too!

16. Spend some time exploring interesting websites. There are sites where you can virtually dissect a frog, view a live feed from an African game preserve, tour the White House, etc.

17. Take time to sit and read. One person can read aloud to everyone else or each person can read a book of their choice. Make popcorn and get comfortable. The winter months are an especially great time for this. A mug of cocoa, a frosty window pane, and a new book!

18. Try something new. Snowshoeing at an area park, rappelling at a local climbing site, a pottery project... take a class or explore

(safely) on your own. A variety of classes can be found through community education, parks and recreation programs and nature centers. State parks also offer an array of nature classes and activities.

19. Ever wondered how they make candy or potato chips or bread? Call to arrange for a factory tour.

20. Take on a community service project. Adopt a cause and find a way to help.... a food drive for a local food shelf, collecting hats, mittens, and warm socks for a homeless shelter, foster a homeless animal, knit a scarf for someone who needs one, the possibilities are endless.

21. Have each child research a possible future career. Check the internet, library, even interview someone in the same field.

22. Visit a college campus. Explore, eat in the cafeteria, check out the bookstore. Talk about the types of degrees and major fields of study offered there.

23. Arrange for a tour of your local fire department or police station. Take homemade cupcakes and thank these public servants for all that they do!

24. Create with papier mache — a piñata or a sculpture or a montage or whatever comes to mind. Paint your finished work or decorate with glue and tissue paper.

25. Write, perform, and videotape your own movie. You'll need a script, setting, and costumes. You can recreate a funny family story or present a retelling of a favorite published book or movie.

There are so many possibilities. Homeschooling is what you make it, so make it FUN!

Our homeschooling style changed over time

"Anyone who stops learning is old, whether at twenty or eighty. Anyone who keeps learning stays young."

– HENRY FORD

I started developing my homeschool philosophy by reading up on education and homeschooling, especially with respect to John Holt and the Montessori method. They are rather opposed to each other in that the Montessori method is quite structured whereas John Holt became more and more a proponent of unschooling over time. What I like about both, though, is the exposure of children to all kinds of learning opportunities and responsibilities, and waiting until they are ready to explore something themselves rather than imposing it on them at a predetermined age.

I spent a lot of time organizing our household in a Montessori way, making sure that everything was at kid level and carefully selected. We had a schedule that worked, putting away all the toys before nap time and bedtime so that the play area was always ready. We did sensory projects and read together and enjoyed plenty of outings to the park.

Then we moved and had a second child, and all that went to smash. Who kept giving us all these wonderful educational toys that were cluttering up the house? Why couldn't I seem to find time to plan activities? And how in the world could I clean up before nap time when my oldest stopped napping just after the second baby was born? Most of all, how could I do it on my own? My husband was suddenly working 80 hours a week trying to get university tenure. We'd moved to Minnesota, thousands of miles away from any of our relatives, and all my new friends so far were other moms with small kids and no time. It was all just a bit overwhelming!

Making friends with other homeschoolers was the absolute best use of my time. Most of the parents in the homeschool social groups I found were veterans of homeschooling, at least compared to me. My oldest wasn't even kindergarten age yet. I really appreciated hearing their perspectives and seeing how different families approached homeschooling and how they all seemed to be doing just fine and were a lot more relaxed than I was about the whole thing. It gave me confidence and support. I especially appreciated the monthly parents' night out, where we could talk about what was and wasn't working and get suggestions for ways to do things differently.

I found myself a bit intimidated by all the amazing things the other homeschool parents seemed to be accomplishing, from starting their kids on second languages at an early age to covering a variety of school subjects that my kids showed little interest in. Looking back, I can see that comparing my family to others was unproductive. In most cases, their kids were older and ready to work on more substantial projects, whereas mine were still small and definitely unready to do any serious work. In addition, having small children is time consuming in and of itself, and I had little perspective on how things would change over time. Fortunately, kids do grow and mature!

I also had grand visions of giving the boys a great educational foundation with a Montessori school up through first grade, and then homeschooling after that. We tried starting our oldest in the local Montessori school at age four, but he wasn't quite ready, and after a month the teachers recommended we try again next year. The next year he was good to go, and I thought we'd have a good three years of formal education, but it was not to be. Even though it was a fine school with lovely teachers, already our oldest was making it clear to us that he really didn't want to be there. Every day he asked if he had to go to kindergarten, and he was happy for the weekends. There wasn't anything wrong with the school or the kids, and he made a couple of great friends right away. It just wasn't for him. We felt the educational experience overrode his dislike of the formal structure, and he went for only one year. He would later encourage our next son to try it, fondly reminiscing about various fun things that his brother would enjoy.

Our middle boy started the same Montessori school at age five, and within a week he'd had his fill of it. Since he was such a social boy I was sure he'd like it, but I was wrong. Like his brother, he made friends and learned a lot. He just didn't like going to school. We asked that he at least finish one semester, and if he still didn't want to go then he could quit. For that entire semester he would ask us about once a week if it was time for him to be done yet, and he was very happy when the term ended.

Our third boy will not be going to school unless he decides he wants to. It may take me a while, but eventually I catch on to what works for each of my kids.

While all this was going on, I continued to educate myself about homeschooling styles and ideas. I went to the Minnesota Homeschoolers Alliance conferences every year, which always had great keynote speakers and useful lectures, and I read everything I could get my hands on. I read books and articles by Sandra Dodd and Peter Gray, Grace Llewellyn and Elizabeth Pantley, Alfie Kohn and Linda Dobson.

I found myself leaning more and more toward unschooling, toward offering experiences and then following what most excited and interested the kids. I also managed to stress myself out trying to be "radical" enough to fit with the radical unschooling ethos, but I just couldn't do it. Radical unschooling is more of a parenting philosophy that emphasizes respect to such a degree that one never insists that a child (or partner) do something he or she doesn't want to do, with the only exceptions being anything that impacts a person's immediate health and safety. The thinking goes that as you model respect for people and the environment your children will learn to respect you and others and their environment. Maybe it works better with some kids than others, or maybe you just have to be really patient for years and years before you see the results. Our oldest was always happy to please, generally willing to help out with tidying up and setting the table and doing a few minutes of workbooks a day. Not so our middle child, who sweetly refused to do any chores, and never said, "Please." In fact, he became downright rude and demanding, and over time it was getting worse rather than better. He was only four, but I could see the same pattern in some older kids we knew, and they weren't getting any better either. I could see that something needed to change—and it needed to be me. So I started insisting on politeness and also on chores. One thing that seemed to get through to him was telling him why: *If you are polite to people, they are more likely to want to help you and give you what you want, and they will enjoy being around you more. If you help clean up the house, your parents will be less stressed out and will have more time to do fun things with you.* He's now extremely polite, and a joy to be around. He'll never love doing chores, and although he complains about them occasionally, he does help out.

Unschooling, especially radical unschooling, is about not forcing kids to study anything or restricting them from doing things. We limit screen time because the research I've seen has shown detrimental effects on developing brains. We do discuss it with the kids, explaining why and working together too figure out how to get them enough time that they feel satisfied while still allowing for plenty of real-world activities. And in the area of studying, it has more to do with me than the kids, but I need at least a little educational structure. I insist that they do a small amount of work in a workbook daily from age seven up, although they do get to choose which subjects they would like to study. The amount of time they spend on their formal work increases as they get older. *Teaching with the Brain in Mind* by Eric Jensen suggests that age plus two is how many minutes a child should be able to sit and work without taking a break, up to a maximum of 30 minutes. This helps focus attention, and it also helps the brain to transfer information to long-term memory during the break. (Moving to a different subject immediately or using social media does not count as a brain break.) Thus our 14-year-old should be able to work for 16-minute stretches, and regularly does. A break could be anything from standing up and stretching, working on an art project, or playing piano, or it could be running around outside for an hour or so, depending on the child and the day. It also depends on the subject and how much they enjoy it. I don't insist that my oldest stop doing math to take a break, because he loves math and that would break his focus. In fact, I let him self-regulate his math completely. He usually spends around 10-15 minutes when it comes to subjects like spelling that don't interest him nearly so much. My middle boy generally uses a timer when doing his workbook, but if he finds an art project to work on he could disappear into it for hours and emerge with an amazing creation. Our youngest is not yet interested in workbooks, and spends his time learning about drawing and Lego gear ratios and woodworking and how to be social with his family and friends.

It might sound like the boys are getting only a few minutes of education a day, but that's not at all the case. Instead we have been delighted to see how much they love to learn when not forced into it. They each pursue their own education independently and approach a variety of subjects with enthusiasm.

One author I have especially appreciated is the psychologist Peter Gray, who writes a blog about unschooling, and the research he's done, not only with American kids, but also with traditional tribes and their childrearing practices. He is a big proponent of democratic schools as well. Reading his perspective on the psychology of learning has helped me to better trust myself and the kids to learn what we need as we need it.

Our homeschooling philosophy will continue to evolve as we grow and learn as a family. Life has gotten busier again as the kids engage in more activities and explore new interests, and I find we need to take time to bond as a family and use downtime to decompress from our busy days. We approach this evolution of homeschooling as a team, everyone working together to figure out how to make things run smoothly and fulfill each person's needs in balance with everyone else's.

TIP: What homeschooling looks like in your family will most likely change and evolve over time, and that is as it should be.

How do I find time for everything?

"Be of good cheer. Do not think of today's failures, but of the success that may come tomorrow. You have set yourselves a difficult task, but you will succeed if you persevere; and you will find a joy in overcoming obstacles. Remember, no effort that we make to attain something beautiful is ever lost."

– HELEN KELLER

Suddenly there are a great many more things to keep track of, and no uninterrupted block of time with the kids away at school to get them done. You may need to get more organized to find time for everything. On the other hand, you may need to let go of some things and just focus on the kids. It's all about managing your priorities, and to do that you have to figure out what they are in the first place. Organize yourself, and then you can work on teaching your kids to manage their time. They will generally follow your example, some kids more than others. Yes, you have to be able to manage the day before they will be able to learn from you. How you do that can be as simple or as complex as you like.

What do I mean by managing priorities? Figure out what it is you most want to focus your limited time and energy on. Is it your relationship with your family? Is it a great education for your children? Is it raising productive and engaged members of society? Spiritual growth? How about feeding the family healthy food? Keeping the house tidy and clean? Doing productive and paying work yourself? Supporting your spouse and prioritizing your relationship? Making sure you have downtime to work on hobbies and keep up your friendships? What about stuff like volunteering, vacations, travel, extended family? Those are all important priorities, and it's easy to get overwhelmed by trying to fit everything in. If you could accomplish one thing in your life, what would it be? Go from there, and then add in the next most important thing to you. Pick your top five, and figure out how to fit them into your life. Stop when you have filled your schedule, don't keep trying to fit in more stuff.

I like to think about it is as choosing a few guiding principles or words that encompass what is most important. My current ones are love, vitality, and abundance. Those cover a lot of ground. Love covers family, friends, learning, and play. Vitality covers exercise, time in nature, health, good food, and a positive attitude. Abundance covers gratitude for what we have, the ability to give to others, and careers and money. Other principles I've enjoyed using as guides have been things like creativity, joy, and giving. Using positive and mindful words like this that can broadly apply to us as a family is important. From there I can organize my day with a positive outlook and a good feel for what needs attention.

In case you're not familiar with Steven Covey's work, I recommend his book *Seven Habits of Highly Effective Families* to help with prioritizing and organizing your time. Sean Covey, Steven's son, has written books for elementary aged kids and for teens that cover the same strategies from the kids' point of view. Another book that I have found really helpful in keeping the house reasonably clean is *Sink Reflections* by Marla Cilley.

One thing we make a point of doing is to include the kids in more chores, so that everyone participates and the adults don't have to do it all. Yes, that adds more work at the beginning, but it makes life easier in the long run. Also, make it clear that there are some tasks that you need to do (and time for yourself that you need to take) when they should occupy themselves. I take an hour every week to talk to my mom on the phone, and I schedule it during their afternoon computer turns while they are watching videos. They also know that if I am in the kitchen cooking dinner, either by myself or with one of the boys, their job is to tidy the living room and set the table. Somehow, though, it often doesn't get done unless my husband is there helping them with it.

I am pretty organized and like to make spreadsheets to keep track of things like my projects and vacation details and such. I have a monthly calendar on the wall for outings, appointments, and classes. On a day to day basis I work from a sticky note that I post in my kitchen. If I can't fit the day's tasks on a two-inch note then I can't fit them into the day, and trying would only stress everyone out. Granted, I write pretty small, and I do two columns. I usually manage to complete somewhere between 12 and 25 tasks, which includes, along with routine items like laundry and meals, things like appointments and outings. When it's the boys' day to do laundry, I don't cross it off my list until after they have it done. That helps me remind them about it so they don't leave their stuff in the washer all day. I love to cross things off my list with a big red marker so I can see how much I've accomplished. In fact, I often write stuff in after I've done it just so I can cross it off and have a visual reminder of my daily achievement. It motivates me to keep going, even on never-ending tasks like laundry. It also helps me remember things from the day before that I might have forgotten if they weren't on a list, like making dentist appointments. When composing the morning's list I check my old post-it to see what might be left over from yesterday.

The boys don't work from post-its, though. We write their daily tasks on a whiteboard. It keeps evolving, and at this point it takes up a lot more room than it once did. I fill it in every morning, asking the boys which chores they are going to do (we hit one room of the house daily Monday through Saturday) and what learning they are going to concentrate on. I also have a space for special projects they want to work on and for outings and other fun things.

To keep track of what we've learned I use a weekly calendar and fill it in after the fact. I keep track of books we've read, classes we've taken, outings we've gone on, workbooks we've done, educational videos we've watched, and other things like practical or social learning, and fine and gross motor skills. It's sort of like a scrapbook, since I will tape in things like tickets, programs, and wristbands from outings. We read so many books that I have begun photocopying all the library receipts and sticking those in so that I don't have to write down every book title. (The receipts fade fairly quickly, which is why I copy them.)

Other people organize their days in other ways. There are plenty of blogs out there with ideas and suggestions for organizing your home and your homeschool. We have friends whose oldest works from a computer calendar. He figures out how much time he needs to spend on each item and how much downtime he needs, and then has his laptop tell him what to do next so he doesn't have to remember it all. That has worked well for him, and he is much less stressed. Some families prefer to have a "command center" with a giant weekly or monthly calendar, and lists of scheduled tasks and assignments. Some families sit down together and work out the daily or weekly schedule, whereas in others one or both parents are in charge of scheduling. I regularly ask our boys whether our schedule is working for them, and adjust it to better suit the family. This does two things: it helps them take more responsibility for their learning and chores because they have a say in it, and when the days go more smoothly I spend less time and effort reminding them to get on to the next thing that needs doing.

As unschoolers, it was much easier when the boys were younger. We hung out, went to playgroups, went to the museum, and spent a lot of time reading, watching documentaries, playing with Legos, and going to parks. We would tidy up before dinner, and then read books before bedtime. Generally, having a framework of time for the day that centered around mealtimes worked well. We would go on any outings in the morning and stay home in the afternoon playing and learning. There wasn't much in the way of time management, and we went a lot of places on the spur of the moment.

Now that they are older and have such a variety of interests, I spend more time nudging them to get things done. My oldest is passionate about math and music, and he is very self-motivated. After the first few weeks of co-op math class at age 11 he has been studying on his own, with only an occasional reminder from me if he needs it. It's a weekly class with about 30 minutes worth of homework a day, and every so often he has to cram a lot of it in during the last 24 hours before class. But that is the exception rather than the rule. The same goes for piano. I don't even bother to ask him if he's practiced because he loves to practice, it's not a chore for him. On the other hand, I do have to remind him about doing some of his chores.

We had to implement a firm rule about getting chores done before computer time, which was the only thing that seemed to motivate them daily. Sometimes they're perfectly happy to pitch in and keep the house clean, but other times not. After having had enough of the dishes filling up every available surface in the kitchen because the dishwasher never got unloaded, mom put her foot down. The dishwasher *must* be unloaded before morning computer turns. Otherwise dinner will be sandwiches, because there is no available space for cooking, and tomorrow's dish situation will be even less appetizing.

Getting things done on the educational front really depends on the task at hand. In general, the boys are good about remembering to do their workbooks and homework, and if there's something they are really into then it can be hard to get them to stop. Over time we have had conversations about getting longer term projects done, and it's one of those talks that seems to come up periodically as the boys mature and take on new tasks. Like me, they often get all fired up about something, spend a bunch of time on it, and then move on to something else they find interesting. If it's just a project they are doing for their own satisfaction, they can come back to it in a week or a month or even a year, and I find they are just as fired up about it the next time around. The time management (and interest management) comes in when we have artificial deadlines imposed such as a piano recital, a classwork due date, or a project to exhibit in a show.

Last year was a real learning experience for my middle son, who took on an ambitious project for the Imagination Fair. He wanted to write a wizard's spell book and make his own binding for it. When we were done it looked amazing, but 80% of the work was done in the last week before the show, 50% of it in the last 24 hours. I had been suggesting that he work on it earlier, and he kept putting it off. I asked if he thought working on the next project a little bit each day might be a good idea, and he definitely saw the value in doing it that way. This year his project was creating a card game. He had to refine the idea, decide how many cards of each kind to make for the best game play, create and print the cards, cut them out, do play testing, and change or add cards to even out some rough spots. He was done with five days to spare, he and did most of the work all on his own.

On the subject of failed projects, I have learned not to say, "I told you so!" when failure occurs. The learning experience is totally lost when someone says that. Any disappointment or upset they might feel about their work is instantly transmuted into righteous anger at you for being smug or not understanding. Instead, I try to ask questions such as, "Do you think it would have worked better if you'd done it another way?" or, "How can we fix that?" Sometimes it's as simple as, "Oops, that didn't work very well, did it?" or, "Are you okay?" Tone of voice is very important, and asking these questions with compassion is very different from asking them sarcastically. I do say things along the lines of, "Told ya!" when they succeed or when they try something I think they'll like. "I knew you could do it—congratulations," "I thought you'd like that," "Good for you for trying," and "I'm glad to see you keep trying even when you get stuck," are all great ways to encourage them.

In summary, organize enough for your own sanity, but don't try to do it all yourself. If you do it all, they won't learn anything except to leave it for mom or dad to do, and you will be exhausted. Then you will have less energy to put into building those important bonds with your kids and your partner. It takes a lot longer in the beginning to teach the kids how to do laundry or manage their time doing projects, and it can be a lot more frustrating than just taking over everything yourself. On the other hand, you will have the satisfaction of seeing your kids taking on more responsibilities, and you will have more energy to let them know just how proud of them you are. And when everyone pitches in and gets things done early, there is more time to do fun things together as a family and with friends.

TOM SAYS: *Homeschooling isn't a panacea, and it isn't for everyone, but it's not as hard as you might think.*

TIP: Figure out what needs doing the most, schedule it into the day, and then fill the rest of it in. Have your kids take responsibility for as much as they are ready for.

How do I find other homeschoolers and activities?

"Change is hardest at the beginning, messiest in the middle and best at the end."
– ROBIN S. SHARMA, *THE LEADER WHO HAD NO TITLE*

You'll need to be proactive at the outset of homeschooling. Look online. Lots of websites have lists of local homeschool groups for you to choose from. Find Facebook and Yahoo groups that feel comfortable to you and ask them for recommendations. That's really the biggest thing—to ask other homeschoolers for suggestions. If you're not sure where to find homeschoolers to begin with, ask anyone who might work with homeschoolers. Check with local community centers, churches or synagogues, libraries, bookstores, attachment parenting support groups, parks and recreation departments, community education programs, or the state department of education. There may be special times reserved for homeschoolers at bowling alleys, rock climbing gyms, trampoline parks, or skating rinks. If you see events advertised specifically for homeschoolers, even if it's not exactly your thing, check them out and meet other people who can give you ideas to work from.

If you can't find a group in your area that is doing things that interest you, form your own group. There are probably other people out there who are in the same boat who would join if only they knew about it. It could be as broad as a playgroup in your area or as specific as a math support group. If you can get the word out to enough people you will start to create your own circle of homeschoolers. If you are in a rural area it might be a small circle, and your get togethers might involve some driving. If you are in an urban area, you will have a pretty big audience to choose from, although there will be competition for times. For several years, Tuesdays seemed to have lots of homeschool activities that we wanted to participate in, and we could never go to all of them. Starting a group that met on Tuesdays wasn't a great idea in that case, and people wanting to start something new usually chose another day. If there are already big groups and you would prefer something smaller, you might create a niche interest group such as food shelf volunteers, aspiring writers, or chess and strategy game buffs. Then advertise your group in places other home-schoolers will look, such as Facebook and Yahoo groups, libraries, community centers, etc.

The biggest thing is not to give up. It may feel like none of the groups is right for your family, and you may even need to go farther afield or online for like-minded people, but that's okay. You don't even have to join a group of homeschoolers for your social outings. You can belong to 4-H or Scouts or the YMCA or whatever else interests you and your kids. The important thing is that you have as much support as your family needs, and enough good friends to make your lives rich.

TIP: Don't wait for others to find you. Be proactive and go find the homeschool group you are looking for. You may have to visit several to find one that's a good fit, or start one yourself.

Resources and References

bookshark.com - Lots of organizational resources for homeschoolers

ck12.org - CK-12 has free resources for Kindergarten through 12th grade

coursera.org - Coursera provides both free and for-credit online university classes

diy.org - A safe site for kids to learn to make things and post their creations

ed.ted.com - TedEd has videos and lesson plans for kids on a wide variety of subjects

edx.org - EdX also provides both free and for-credit online university classes

homeschool.com - A great place to find homeschool resources, methods and daily timelines

HomeSchoolResourceSp.com - Homeschool testing and resources

khanacademy.org - Khan Academy provides free resources from Kindergarten up

mheducation.com - Redbird is a math program developed by Stanford University

topscience.org - TOPS math and science resources

wired.com/2015/02/silicon-valley-home-schooling - Wired article on DIY/Maker Homeschooling

The 7 Habits of Happy Kids, Sean Covey & Stacy Curtis (illustrator), Simon & Schuster Books for Young Readers (September 16, 2008), 4-8 years

The 7 Habits of Highly Effective Families, Steven R. Covey, St. Martin's Griffin (October 1, 1997)

The 7 Habits of Highly Effective Teens, Sean Covey, Touchstone, Updated Edition (May 27, 2014)

Free to Learn: Why Unleashing the Instinct to Play Will Make Our Children Happier, More Self-Reliant, and Better Students for Life, Peter Gray, Basic Books, 1st Edition (February 10, 2015)

How Math Works, Carol Vorderman, Readers Digest (August 6, 1996)

Hoyle's Rules of Games: The Essential Family Guide to Card Games, Board Games, Parlor Games, New Poker Variations, and More, Albert H. Morehead, Geoffrey Mott-Smith, and Philip D. Morehead, Berkley, 3rd Revised and Updated Edition (December 1, 2001)

The I Hate Mathematics! Book, Marilyn Burns, Little, Brown Books for Young Readers, 1st Edition (July 30, 1975)

The Leader Who Had No Title: A Modern Fable on Real Success in Business and in Life, Robin Sharma, Free Press, 1st Edition (December 28, 2010)

Math Curse, Jon Scieszca and Lane Smith, Viking, Library Binding Edition (October 1, 1995) 3-7 years

The Number Devil: A Mathematical Adventure, Hans Magnus Enzensberger, Rotraut Susanne Berner & Michael Henry Helm, Picador (August 18, 2010) (For 11-15-year-olds, but my kids loved it starting around age 7)

Sink Reflections, Marla Cilley, Bantam, Reissue Edition (October 1, 2002)

Chaos to Clean in 31 Easy BabySteps, Marla Cilley, FLYLADY AND COMPANY, 1st Edition (2017) FlyLady.net

Teaching with the Brain in Mind, Eric Jensen S.J., Association for Supervision & Curriculum Development, Revised 2nd Edition (January 1, 2005)

Overcoming Objections

How do I get friends and family on board?

"If you find yourself engaged in an argument that only stirs anger in the heart, quickly make peace and carry on."
– SUZY KASSEM, *RISE UP AND SALUTE THE SUN*

I've been fairly lucky in having a lot of support from my husband, but not everyone starts out with familial support. If your partner needs persuading, look at the facts, consult studies, talk about how prestigious universities like Stanford are now seeking out homeschooled students because of their maturity and self-motivation, and have him or her meet other homeschooling families, especially ones similar in style to yours. And keep bringing up the ways in which you see it benefitting your child and your family. Keep *The Well-Adjusted Child* and other good books on homeschooling around the house for when you need to cite actual facts. It may take a while. Sometimes it helps to have your partner play devil's advocate and tell you why it would be good while you take their position. That can help not only with seeing the other's point of view, but it also helps bring up pros and cons you might not have thought of.

TOM SAYS: *Being a homeschooler doesn't mean you can't or shouldn't be active in trying to reform and/or improve public schooling. Join the local school board, vote in all your local elections, and try to make public school a better place for all kids.*

Once you have the support of your partner, it's a lot easier to handle doubts and questions from other people. My best suggestion is to see if they are open to learning more about homeschooling, and if so, take a little time to educate them on the benefits. Talk to them about their concerns. Keep in mind that in general people feel they have the best interests of your kids (and theirs) at heart and are trying to help. Also, I have found that it's much better to talk about specific benefits to your own kids, rather than attacking the school system or the educational choices of other people.

When our boys were younger I would go on about homeschooling and the school system until people's eyes glazed over, or until they became defensive about the education they received and the fact that their kids were in traditional school. I was convinced everyone should be homeschooling. Now that I've had more time to see how things are working (or not) for our kids and their cohorts, both in school and outside of it, my attitudes have become more nuanced.

Traditional schools works well for plenty of families, and often it's the only viable choice for them. I can also see that many of the objections that other people raised came out of genuine concern and also from trying to shore up their confidence in their own choices. However, when I talk about tailoring educational experiences to the child, people often really get that.

My parents were both a bit dubious about homeschooling— maybe more than a bit—but they were willing to at least listen and to learn about it. I've shared numerous books and articles with them, and over time they have come to be big supporters. The biggest objection I had to overcome has to do with socialization, because they weren't particularly worried about our ability to help the children learn. I think one thing that was especially helpful was having them visit and participate in our homeschool activities. They could meet other homeschooling parents and kids, see the social interactions, and experience the educational opportunities we presented during the course of a week. Granted, we did more fun stuff like go to museums and on other outings simply because grandma or grandpa was here, but they got a pretty good sense of what our days are like. Now they send me resources they think the boys will like and interesting studies about learning and education. Recently my dad told me that he's very glad we decided to homeschool the boys.

It also helps to remind yourself that conventional school is always an option. It can be reassuring to others to let them know that if you decide homeschooling isn't working for your kids, you can always send them to school. "Have you considered sending them (back) to school?" can be answered with, "We reevaluate their progress and development on a regular basis to find the best educational experience for them," or even, "If we feel school would be better for them, then that's what we'll do."

Sadly, there will always be naysayers, whether it is about homeschooling or something else. If they are not interested in learning about your point of view, you may have to avoid discussing the subject with them. That has been the case with a few of our relatives, although we are fortunate that not very many of them feel that way. Surround yourself with people who will give you the support and ideas and help that you need to make a successful go of homeschooling.

On the other hand, don't discount every negative comment before examining it for useful information. It can be hard to take when it comes in that form, but I've been motivated to do things that were good for our family as a result of harsh comments. I wish it hadn't taken me so long to realize that our son needed a good therapist for his social anxiety, but I am thankful someone was blunt enough to get the point across.

TIP: Be patient with others, and be confident in yourself. Talk about the specific benefits of homeschooling, ask others about their concerns, provide facts, and let it drop if someone becomes defensive or obnoxious. You can come back to it later when emotions aren't running high.

What if I don't have a degree?

"We have forgotten that children are designed by nature to learn through self-directed play and exploration, and so, more and more, we deprive them of freedom to learn, subjecting them instead to the tedious and painfully slow learning methods devised by those who run the schools."

– PETER GRAY, *FREE TO LEARN*

This really breaks down into two separate questions: "What if I don't have a teaching degree?" and "What if I don't have a college degree?"

The first one is the easiest to handle. A teaching degree does not magically bestow you with wisdom and knowledge that you then pass on to the students. A teaching degree is primarily about learning classroom management, and you do not need that to homeschool. Lesson planning is something that you can pick up fairly easily if you want to teach actual lessons, or you can spend money on a curriculum that already has the lessons planned. While they tend to be expensive, it's a lot cheaper than a degree, and it doesn't require years of extra schooling. For those who want to spend a little more time looking around, there are plenty of resources online, including free lesson plans and useful materials.

If you prefer a more organic approach to learning, lesson plans aren't necessary at all. When we find a subject that interests us, we pursue it. Our family collects books, so in many cases we can go straight to the bookshelf and find something to get us started. After that it's the library, the internet, the science museum, or the history museum. We get ideas and then go after them, for as long as it interests us. Sometimes finding an answer to a simple question leads us to related subjects, and sometimes that answer is all that's needed.

Deschooling for Teachers

This short piece was written by a friend of mine, Susie, who was a licensed teacher, but had to learn how not to teach her children the way she would teach a class.

"For those who are thinking about homeschooling, but doubt that they can...

We didn't start homeschooling my son until he was seven, and even then, he really wasn't ready. Although obviously very intelligent, his skills did not translate to paper and pencil learning. So I pushed. There were tears, and it sucked. This was not how I wanted things to be, so I backed off, way off.

"The first year that we did standardized testing, I had to read the whole test to him. The year after, he scored at or below grade level on everything. Still, I trusted that when his brain was ready he would learn what he needed. The maximum amount of time that I would spend with him on directed teaching per day was one hour. All other learning was completely self-directed.

"This year, in third grade, he was finally able to read all of the directions and lessons by himself. He is nine. Within the short eight months that we've been schooling this year, he has blossomed. Last year, he was barely reading, and certainly not doing it for fun. This year, he plows through chapter books in two days. The maximum amount of time we spend on written, non-self-directed work is 90 minutes. We formal school this way an average of three to four days a week. Most days consist of hours and hours of playing outside.

"We just completed his yearly testing using the Peabody exam. His overall score has doubled since last year. He is above grade level on everything but math. In math, he is exactly where he should be. My non-reader just a year ago is now at a seventh grade comprehension level. This progression has been 100% him, and 100% me backing off and allowing him to be a kid and grow at his own pace and pursuing things of his own interest (robots, Legos, inventions, animals).

"Had he been in the school system, I strongly feel that he would not have had these successes. You cannot force children to learn when they are not ready. Testing does not indicate intelligence. A long school day with hours of sitting is not conducive to learning.

"As a licensed teacher, I thought I knew all there was to know about these things, but no. I've learned more over the last three years schooling and unschooling my child than I did during my years in college learning theory and application.

"So if you are thinking that you can't do it, that it won't be enough, that you need a degree to teach, that it will be too complicated, I'm here to tell you that you absolutely can, that it will be enough, that you don't need a degree, and that it does not need to be complicated."

A college degree is not essential either. In fact, even having a good high school education is not essential. What is important is dedication to learning. A good book on the subject is *Family Matters* by David Guterson, which goes into the studies done on the successes of various students. The main takeaway here is that the most important key to any student's success in education is the dedication of their parents to their kids' education. Not the parents' education level, and not the kind of school or homeschool they choose for their kids. As an example, think about stories of high achieving second generation immigrants whose parents not only didn't have a good education in their country of origin, but didn't even speak English. What they did have was dedication to their children's success in school, and that made all the difference.

Some states may have more hoops for you to jump through if you don't have a college degree, but above all know that you are fully capable of helping your children learn. Although Minnesota has now changed its statute regarding the degree requirements of homeschool parents, when we first moved here we were required to provide copies of our diplomas. For those without diplomas there were different requirements and more oversight from the state, but that didn't stop plenty of people without degrees from homeschooling.

Education is not a static thing, and teaching children does not mean you have to have every fact at your fingertips. In fact, if you knew everything, it might even stunt your children's ability to become independent learners. Why bother looking something up or figuring out how to do it when mom or dad already knows? Good thing parents don't know everything! Instead, relish the fact that together you can explore geography, the world of physics, the Roman Empire, a foreign language, or Lego robotics. Then you can teach a more important lesson: How to be inquisitive, to know how to find what you want to learn, and question what you think you know. By doing this, you will also create bonds of trust and appreciation in your kids, which will prove an enormous help through the trials and tribulations of growing up.

John Holt's Requirements for Teaching

"We can sum up very quickly what people need to teach their own children. First of all, they have to like them, enjoy their company, their physical presence, their energy, foolishness, and passion. They have to enjoy all their talk and questions, and enjoy equally trying to answer those questions. They have to think of their children as friends, indeed very close friends, have to feel happier when they are near and miss them when they are away. They have to trust them as people, respect their fragile dignity, treat them with courtesy, take them seriously. They have to feel in their own hearts some of their children's wonder, curiosity, and excitement about the world. And they have to have enough confidence in themselves, skepticism about experts, and willingness to be different from most people, to take on themselves the responsibility for their children's learning. But that is about all that parents need. Perhaps only a minority of parents have these qualities. Certainly some have more than others. Many will gain more as they know their children better; most of the people who have been teaching their children at home say that it has made them like them more, not less. In any case, these are not qualities that can be taught or learned in a school, or measured with a test, or certified with a piece of paper."

Teach Your Own, John Holt, Da Capo Press, First Paperback Edition (April 2003)

TIP: Find out what the legal requirements are in your state, and give your children the education you want for them. Remember that teaching them how to learn and find resources is more important than having specific knowledge before you start.

How will they learn anything?

"We were lucky enough to grow up in an environment where there was always much encouragement to children to pursue intellectual interests; to investigate what ever aroused curiosity."

– ORVILLE WRIGHT

Humans are built for learning. Babies don't learn to talk and to walk because we've sent them to school or put them through a learning program. In fact, forcing babies to walk before they're ready and putting academic pressures on children at too young an age has been shown to be counterproductive. Children learn because their brains and bodies impel them toward it. You can't stop them from learning, although they may learn things that aren't intended, as mentioned in *Dumbing Us Down*. If learning has become an externally imposed chore, the natural impulse to question and be curious can be squashed, and education becomes dull, tedious, and stressful.

This is where deschooling plays such an important role. And if you've been homeschooling and find yourself with kids reacting this way, you may even need to deschool from homeschooling. Or you may need to work with your kids to find a better way. My kids are teaching me all the time about how they learn.

My oldest did not leap into reading at a young age. He learned his alphabet earlier than I expected and knew a few words, but for him reading took time. The Montessori school sent home Kindergarten reading homework, which he plodded through, reading out loud to us. But it wasn't a joy for him. So we found fun and easy books for him like *Ricky Riccotta* and *Captain Underpants* by Dave Pilkey. We wound up mostly reading them to him as he followed along. We've always read to the boys, from *Winnie the Pooh* to *The Boxcar Children* to *Harry Potter* to Bill Bryson and Agatha Christie, and we rotate who gets to choose so that everyone hears something they enjoy. I also make sure I get a turn to choose, so that I continue to be motivated to read.

It seemed to be taking a very long time for our oldest to learn to read fluently. Our second son picked up reading on his own very quickly, and soon surpassed his brother. By second grade he was reading at a sixth grade level, while his older brother skimmed through comic books. I was a bit worried, but I had heard plenty of anecdotes from older homeschoolers about their non-readers suddenly picking up *Harry Potter* in sixth grade and devouring the whole series, or learning to read by playing Minecraft. So we let him keep reading comic books. I found as many interesting graphic novels as I could for him at the library, he checked out the large collection of Classic Comics that my dad has, and we kept reading aloud. I was reading the *Harry Potter* series to them at the rate of one per year, so that their maturity level kept pace with the intensity level of the books. A new one arrived from Santa yearly. When I started on the fifth book, both boys decided to go back and read the fourth book to remind themselves what happened, and suddenly both of them were plowing through the whole series as fast as they could. Somewhere between the ages of nine and eleven seems to be a magic age of reading for a lot of kids, and homeschooling allowed us to let this happen naturally. He wasn't "failing" reading, his brain just wasn't ready for it yet. When it was, he leaped into reading with enthusiasm because we hadn't been forcing it on him. The way the school system is set up, kids have to be reading fluently by fourth grade to be able to keep up with their other subjects, and those who aren't ready yet or who have learning disabilities often fall by the wayside. I suspect that if he had been in conventional school he would hate reading the way a lot of people hate math, and for many of the same reasons. Now he's steadily making his way through math books his father read after graduate school, like *Euler: Master of Us All* and *Here's Looking at Euclid*, and he has read the whole *Harry Potter* series at least three times.

Likewise, there are a lot of kids who don't do well with geometry or algebra until their brains have matured. My high school geometry teacher said he saw this a lot over his years of teaching. He started every year with a bunch of new sophomores, many of whom just didn't "get" geometry. Over the course of the year, as their brains matured, almost all of them would suddenly snap into it and understand what was being taught. I didn't think much of it at the time. It was not something that applied to me, as I was taking geometry a year later than most students because of switching schools. Now I have to wonder why in the world you would subject so many students to something they aren't going to understand anyway until partway through the year? Just put it off until they're ready, and then they can learn it much more naturally, not to mention efficiently, and maybe even enjoy it in the bargain.

Bear in mind that not all kids will suddenly start reading fluently or understanding math. What homeschooling does is give them a chance to learn at their own pace without being pressured to keep up with the pack. Those kids who are developmentally ready for what is being presented to them will have an easier time, and those who have actual disabilities will have a teacher—you—who understands their needs and can help them find the resources or therapy or tutors they need. Patience and one-on-one time go a very long way.

Learning really is a natural and enjoyable process. If you have the right mindset you can help your kids to understand this. When they ask questions, don't be afraid to say, "I don't know, let's find out!" Help them with their enquiries and encourage them to pursue their own interests. It's always easier to learn something you're interested in than something you find tedious, so model that for them. What do *you* like to learn about? Let your kids see you figuring out a complicated recipe or a computer programming language or a musical instrument, anything that you enjoy knowing more about. If they see that learning isn't just for kids, and isn't just applied to "schoolwork," they will be much more likely to grow up with a love of learning. Good resources for understanding learning are John Holt's book, *Learning All the Time*, and Peter Gray's book, *Free to Learn*.

 TIP: You can't stop people from learning. We are all programmed from birth to learn constantly. Help your kids understand how they learn best and where to find resources, and that learning should be fun, interesting, and relevant.

What if they hate math?
What if I hate math?

"Children must be taught how to think, not what to think."

- MARGARET MEAD

Don't worry, math can be fun. And even if you can't quite bring yourself to enjoy it, there is no reason you can't find ways for your kids to learn to like it. There are lots of ways you can approach making it interesting and useful. For elementary math, play math games like Math Dice, Equate, Allowance, or Monopoly. Have them help with adding up the prices of the groceries in your cart so you can stay within your budget, and the first one who correctly figures out how much change you'll get back can keep that change. Try having a weekly "candy math" day. Kim Jaworski, whose suggestions I included in chapter two, came up with this idea to make learning math practical as well as fun. Working on fractions this week? Buy a chocolate bar. Measure it, talk about the different ways it could be divided. Figure out if you get to eat more if you have 2/3 or 3/5 of it. Then divide it up and eat it. Bags of small candies can be used similarly, or divided by color to look at statistics and probability. There are lots of possibilities.

When my middle son was learning multiplication, he declared that he hated math. This baffled me. I like math. My husband and my oldest have brains that grasp numbers very quickly, and they can do complex calculations in their heads easily. Our oldest thrives on math and has always loved numbers, and I thought our middle boy enjoyed it, too. When I really sat down and thought about it, though, I realized that I had hated math as a kid, thinking I was no good at it. Why? Because of the pressure of memorizing and having to know and regurgitate facts on timed tests. I am not quick when it comes to remembering math facts. I am very accurate, but I can't whip out the seven times table and never could. I was the only person in my fourth grade class who couldn't finish the addition test in the time allotted. Ever. I never got to move on to subtraction or multiplication because I was still doing addition every week, for that entire year. To make the whole thing more humiliating, there was a display above the chalkboard where the entire class could see who was progressing and who wasn't. Some students even lapped me and had started on harder tests while I was still struggling with the first one. Nobody ever told me that I was approaching it wrong, that whereas checking your work is very important on a regular test, on a timed test it is not a priority. So I became convinced I was bad at math, and so did my teacher. Sadly, I had the same teacher in sixth grade, and she was still convinced I was bad at math. It wasn't until I hit classes where accuracy and not speed counted, like algebra and geometry, that my higher math brain kicked in and I rose to the top of the class. It also helped that those teachers didn't assume I wasn't going to understand anything.

This insight helped hugely with my middle son when I sat down with him and explained that he was not his brother and shouldn't compare himself to his brother. That his brain is more like mine, and we just have to work harder to memorize numbers, and to use our skills to work out numbers we haven't memorized. On the other hand, we prefer advanced mathematical concepts. One reason it surprised me when he declared his hatred for math was because he had loved math concepts as early as the second grade. He especially liked watching videos on complex mathematical ideas such as Sierpinski's triangle and the hotel with an infinite number of full rooms that has to make room for an infinitely large busload of new guests. Honestly, these are concepts I didn't even run into in college, and I only learned them with the boys as we were watching TedEd and Vi Hart videos. Here's a boy who spent an hour carefully drawing and coloring in a Sierpinski triangle (taking up three pages taped together) who said he hated math.

Having someone to commiserate with when he was struggling to memorize the multiplication table made such a difference. I shared with him a bunch of my tricks, but he may never be particularly fast at multiplication. Now he enjoys trying out different methods of long division and multiplication to see what makes the most sense to him and gets him the correct answer consistently. And he tells me he likes math. In fact, he was quite surprised recently when I mentioned what he'd said a couple of years ago about hating math. As long as he has confidence that he can figure things out—and tries instead of giving up—I am satisfied.

Recently I had to laugh thinking back on my fourth grade teacher. I was talking to a mortgage broker about refinancing our house. I had done my homework and I understood all the terms that she was discussing, so I could follow the numbers just fine. She commented that I must be really good at math. Yes, yes, I am. In things that really count in life, like mortgages and interest payments and budgets. But you couldn't have proved it by talking with my elementary school teacher.

This section really applies to any subject, not just math. Does history bore you to tears? Yeah, me too. That's because history textbooks are filled with facts, not stories. History is a story, in fact, many, many stories, all interwoven. Watch historical dramas, read the *My America* series or, if the kids are old enough, Nathan Hale's graphic novels of American history. Bill Bryson makes history pretty funny, and his books cover subjects as widely varied as the English language, science, and architecture. Learn about the people in history rather than insisting on dry memorization of dates and events. Read books on mythology and talk about how stories from a country's past can inform its citizens' ethos today. Find somebody who loves history and spend time discussing it with them. Apply these strategies to any subject, including those you actually enjoyed in school.

TOM SAYS: *On the other hand, if you have little patience for stories, history can be about concepts and ideas. There are lots of ways to engage with any given subject; find one that interests you.*

 TIP: You can homeschool whether you loved school, hated school, or were somewhere in the middle. You don't have to be the one to teach every single thing, and you might even discover you enjoy a subject when you're not being forced to memorize a boring textbook.

Isn't homeschooling expensive?

"Learning and education are a normal part of everyday life and do not need a vast expensive bureaucracy to force them to happen."
— **KYTKA HILMAR-JEZEK,** *99 QUESTIONS AND ANSWERS ABOUT UNSCHOOLING*

Do you have access to a library and the internet, to a park or community center? You're set! Even if you don't have internet access at home, you can join the library and use their computers. On the other hand, if you have internet service but no local library, you can find pretty much anything you need online. Go outside or to the community center for physical skills, and check out free classes to see if there are any that suit your family.

Our library system offers a lot of free resources beyond just books. They host book clubs for various ages, story time for preschoolers (including an evening pajama story time), film festivals, music events, science activities, a summer reading program, author events, free tutoring, and much more. Our boys have even taken a couple of free pottery classes put on by the prestigious Northern Clay Center at the library.

You can buy fancy curricula if you really want to, but it's not necessary. In fact, it may be the worst thing you can do, at least right off the bat. It's very disheartening to get all excited about something and spend a bunch of money on it, only to have the kids hate it. Maybe it doesn't work for their learning style or maybe they find it boring, or maybe they hate it because it's too much like school and they've had enough of someone else telling them which things they need to memorize. Or just maybe they hate it because it was expensive and you *really* want them to use it. If you've spent a lot of money on it, you're invested in having them love it, or at least complete the darn thing. Believe me, the harder I try to make the kids do something the more resistance I get. Instead, work together to find things that are interesting and free, or at least inexpensive. There are a ton of them out there. It helps if both you and the kids find them interesting because it means you can share the excitement of learning, although ultimately it has to be something they want to learn about.

Moving on to a related topic: How does one afford to stay at home to homeschool? Well, there are lots of ways. In many families one parent works and the other stays home. Sure, it's often the mom who stays home, but not always. I've known a couple of dads who stay home full time to be with the kids. And yes, this can mean a big cut in the paycheck. I stay home while my husband works, and we don't eat out very often. On the bonus side, I can now cook a much wider variety of food than I could when I was working full time, plus the kids are learning how to cook. Our oldest loves to bake and is starting a business selling his cookies. We don't do Disney vacations, we take road trips to see family, with interesting museums and national parks thrown in. Our science museum membership does double duty because our museum is part of the ASTC network, so it gives us entry into other museums all over the country. Since we are always looking for learning opportunities, visits to the relatives are an integral part of our homeschooling plan.

There are many other iterations of homeschooling that are possible. Both parents can work full time but on a staggered schedule so that there is always someone home. One or both parents can work part time. Single parents can and do homeschool. It takes a lot of work—and often help time wise and with cash from relatives—and plenty of single parent families are making homeschooling work. It also helps when the kids are old enough to be responsible for themselves and their homework without having a parent directing their every move. Kids will step up to the challenge. They are capable of far more than our current culture gives them credit for.

The most important thing to remember is that if it's something you really want to do, you will find a way. Bringing mindfulness to your decision and to your budget, rather than coming from a place of worry, will help you stay calm and see the possibilities. Homeschoolers are very creative at finding and inventing free or inexpensive learning opportunities for their kids, and also very creative at devising ways to pay for things. There are a lot of homeschoolers who work from home, or who have created businesses around homeschooling to help them cover the bills. There are bloggers, people who design and sell curricula or transcript journals, and people who offer testing services to other homeschoolers. Some people start their own cottage businesses doing crafts, or they consult, tutor, or do contract work. There are also parents who work outside the home but do an early morning or late evening shift so as to be home during the majority of the day. Yes, you might spend more money on homeschooling than you would sending the kids to public school, but you might not. It's a lot less than sending them to private school or hiring a personal tutor. It may well be less than you would spend on a fancy vacation, a boat, or new smartphones for the family. As a bonus, all the peer pressure to buy name-brand clothing and shoes will probably disappear. Just decide what your priorities are so that you can feel that every dollar put toward education is money well spent.

TIP: Homeschooling doesn't have to be expensive. Make a budget and stick to it. When homeschooling is your priority, other things become less important, and you can almost always find a way.

What if all they want to do is play video games?

*"Normally it's hard to **stop** happy, satisfied people from trying to learn more about themselves and the world, or from trying to do a job of which they can feel proud. The desire to do as little as possible is ... a sign that something is wrong."*

– ALFIE KOHN, *UNCONDITIONAL PARENTING*

Gaming is a question that a lot of people worry about when considering homeschooling. First, consider the facts of what's happening now. Are you worried that your kids *might* play games all day if left to their own devices, or are they *actually* spending every spare moment playing video games? Do they really have that much spare time in which to play? In other words, are they at school eight hours a day, plus homework and extracurriculars, and squeezing in games whenever they can? Or are they home and gaming 12-15 hours a day, barely stopping to eat? In most cases, it's likely not as much gaming as you think. I find that my own worries about screen time tend to blow things out of proportion, and I need to be mindful about what the reality actually is. The kids are generally not gaming as much as my fears make it out to be, often watching educational videos during their turns, and you may find the same. On the other hand, if it truly is enough to worry about, something is going on that should be addressed. We discuss screen-time's effects on physical and mental health, and even the addictiveness of some kinds of gaming and of social media with the boys so that they are cognizant of why we don't allow unlimited computer time in our house. We don't own a television and although we do have Netflix we only watch movies in the evening after dinner. We do make exceptions from time to time, such as when the kids are sick.

After assessing what's actually going on, find out why the games are so compelling. What need is that filling? Are they playing video games nonstop to escape from stress, bullying, or other kid worries? Are they introverts who need more downtime after a day full of social interaction? Do they feel powerless in other areas of life and need an arena in which they are in control? Are they on the Aspergers-autism spectrum, where the structured nature of gaming is soothing to them after the chaos of daily life? Are they out of the habit of finding alternate ways to amuse themselves? Is it social gaming, where it fills a social need? Or are the games simply fun?

Now try to figure out ways other than gaming to get those needs met. If school is stressing them out, or overstimulating them, you already know my answer to that. Keep in mind, too, that school is often the culprit in feelings of powerlessness. If you take school out of the equation, the need to immerse themselves in another world where they have the power to determine their own fate may quickly peter out.

Gaming may merely be another form of decompressing from the day. What do you and your partner do to decompress after a long day? Do you watch television or check social media? Some people read, exercise, cook, play board games, practice yoga, or do crossword puzzles. These are all coping strategies for an over-busy world, and different things work for different people. Gaming fills the same mental need. Try introducing new strategies to the family as methods for decompressing from a long day and see what takes. Maybe you'll find something new yourself, and you might even find something the whole family can do together. My husband introduced sudoku and kenken games to the kids, and now our oldest loves to do them at bedtime to quiet his brain before sleeping. We took an improv theater class last spring as a family, and now we like to play silly games we learned there to bond and relax. The boys do Legos with their dad, I read to them, and we all play board games together. Each of these fills a slightly different need, from laughing and playing together to quietly concentrating on building things to calming your brain before sleeping.

Also, see if adding in new things to do will help if the main cause of excessive gaming is not having anything to do. These days it's a lot harder to just send the kids outside because there's nobody out there to play with. You might need to put in some extra work to help them find friends and groups to spend time with. Work with your kids to find toys, games, projects, art, anything that will spark their interests and get them back in the habit of amusing themselves rather than being amused.

For some perspective on gaming and the autistic brain, check out Danny Raede's website, AspergerExperts.com. Video gaming can be a coping mechanism for the anxiety caused by the brain overreacting to ordinary stimuli. Raede has a number of suggestions, including using a responsibility agreement once you have discussed gaming and figured out what needs it fills. Building connections with your kids and helping them find good friends also removes some of the need to numb the brain with video games.

When gaming is just for fun, or if it is filling a social need, support your children in finding regular times to play. If they know they will always get their gaming, even if it has to be put off occasionally, they are less likely to try to squeeze in every moment they can. You might even schedule binge days every so often, if it doesn't disrupt the family too much. On the other hand, if that makes them cranky, hungry, and lashing out at people, you can point that out (at a later time) and talk about how it doesn't seem to be good for their mental or physical health, and certainly isn't good for the health of the family. Find a balance that works for your family, which will be different than what works for other families.

You will need to decide together how much screen time is appropriate for your family, and what level of virtual violence is acceptable. The American Academy of Pediatrics (AAP) used to suggest no more than two hours a day for school-aged children, including computers, tablets, and phones. They have since made more nuanced suggestions, which you can find at HealthyChildren.org. Bear in mind that Steve Jobs, one of the founders of Apple, did not let his own children have iPads. The AAP also recommends at least an hour of exercise every day, and we have exercise and outside time on our daily chart of activities.

The regulation of violence in video games is going to have to be based on the comfort level of your family. The studies are mixed as to whether violence in video games and movies contributes to violence in real life. Some have found a strong correlation, whereas others have not. We don't let the kids play realistic first-person shooter games. Our oldest did spend several months playing Minecraft games that were first-person shooter, but we felt the graphics were not too disturbing. That interest seems to have worn off, and now he's spending more time programming and playing strategic games.

Finally, play games *with* your kids! If you want to know why they are obsessed with Minecraft or whatever the newest popular game is, sit down with them and play together. You might find a bonding point over games and even enjoy family game nights together. At the very least, you will have a better perspective on your kids' interests. And sometimes having a parent interested in the game might make their own interest wane, especially if they are trying to be defiant and rebellious through their gaming activities. Our computer is in the living room, and most game turns take place there, with the whole family able to watch and comment if someone is playing a particularly interesting game. One thing I learned from playing together is that telling them to get off the computer *right now* is useless and annoying. Now I can see where they are in a game, keep them posted on how much time they have left, and remind them to save the game at the end of their level. All of us are less frustrated that way.

TIP: Video games are not inherently good or bad, and they may fill an important need. Be open to finding out why games are important, join in playing, offer other alternatives to fill some needs, and discuss your family values around things like exercise, social time, and violence in video games.

What if my kids argue with me all the time?

"We need to get in the habit of asking ourselves a very specific question: 'If that comment [or action] I just [did] to my child had been done to me...would I feel unconditionally loved?' It's not terribly complicated to perform this sort of imaginative reversal, but to do so on a regular basis can be nothing short of transformative."

– ALFIE KOHN, *UNCONDITIONAL PARENTING*

"Cultivating strong family bonds is a natural side effect of homeschooling as we pursue our interests, share chores and simply enjoy one another's company."

– LAURA GRACE WELDON, *FREE RANGE LEARNING*

If your kids are arguing with you constantly, look at what you are arguing about. If you're considering homeschooling but are hesitating because you have a lot of friction in your family about getting ready for school on time, having homework done, and behavior problems in school, I would say that's an argument for homeschooling rather than against it. I have seen many families whose stress levels, and consequently their argument frequency, have gone way down when school was taken out of the equation. I have also seen kids who went from being very disrespectful of their parents (learned from kids at school) to being kind and helpful and all-around nice people after making friends in the homeschool community. If all your friends like their parents, it's easier to feel that way yourself.

Another thing to look at is compliance. If you feel like you are always laying down the law and then facing a lot of resistance, consider changing your parenting strategy. I recommend *How To Talk So Kids Will Listen*, *Kid Cooperation*, *Unconditional Parenting*, and other books in that genre. On the other hand, if it's more important to you that your kids obey you than that there be an atmosphere of collaboration in your house, you may not find what you need in this section. I have no idea how to make kids obey unquestioningly without using emotional or physical coercion, which is something I work hard to avoid. I also saw the backlash of that firsthand while growing up, because I had several friends with authoritarian parents. Authoritarian parents rigidly demand obedience, often laying down the law without any discussion of why those rules are important, and using harsh punishments or shaming. "Because I said so" or even, "Because our religion says so" are authoritarian answers. The kids who didn't outright rebel against these rules were quiet and well behaved any time there were authority figures around, but often got up to all kinds of sneaky shenanigans as soon as they went unobserved. If your moral compass is externally imposed, it won't help you make good decisions when you're on your own.

Overly permissive parents also don't end up with kids who have a good moral compass. Permissive parenting goes the other direction, allowing too much freedom and not imposing enough rules, sometimes with warmth and caring, other times through neglect. Kids from permissive families often end up feeling very entitled, not understanding why they should take other people's wants and needs into account.

Alfie Kohn in *Unconditional Parenting* says the best way to learn to make good decisions is to be allowed to make decisions - as a parent, let your kids make as many of their own decisions as you can, and *help them through* the consequences of those decisions. That doesn't just mean decisions we don't care about, like what color sippy cup or backpack they want, but also as many decisions that don't directly affect the family's health and safety as possible. This may sound like permissive parenting, but the execution is very different. The whole point is to help children learn the consequences of their behavior in as loving a manner as possible, neither punishing them for making the "wrong" choice nor rewarding them for making the "right" choice.

It's a delicate balance, not letting kids get away with bad behavior while giving responsibility, being forgiving of mistakes, and being willing to discuss the purpose of rules and the consequences of both good and bad behavior. Asking open-ended questions and then really listening to your kids can help pinpoint problem areas so you can help them work through dilemmas and areas of friction.

It's very important to make the focus of your parenting be unconditional love. In the moment, be as loving as you can. Try to remember the mindful parenting rules: notice your feelings when in conflict with your child, pause and respond calmly, and listen to your child. If you say you love the kids but not the behavior, it doesn't mean anything if you withdraw that love until they comply. That's just using love and attention as your reward, which is more insidious and emotionally damaging than if you offered physical bribes for good behavior. Explain how their behavior affects other people, in a loving way, because you really do want the best for them and for them to grow up into wonderful and responsible human beings. Resist forcing them to do (or not do) things unless absolutely necessary for health and safety. Imagine a spouse or friend who wanted you to do something. How would you like to be treated in the same situation?

Go easy on yourself, as well. None of us are perfect, and there will always be times when we react instead of reflect with our kids (and partners, too). Be willing to apologize, own up to your behavior and how it might have affected the other person, and then listen to their side of the story. If you know there are situations that consistently push you over the edge, try to anticipate them and have a plan in place. I have an image of myself as a calm and patient parent without a lot of buttons to push, so I am occasionally blindsided by my reactions when one of those few buttons does get pushed. A smugly defiant kid pushes buttons from my childhood, and I have learned to turn that kid over to my husband as soon as possible to keep from becoming irrationally angry. If he's not home, I take a time out in my room to do some deep breathing, read a book or call a good friend who can talk me down. I know it's a developmental stage that all my kids went through around the age of five, and will likely hit again in the teens, but I am so happy our youngest has finally turned six and seems to be through it.

When kids know that they have parents who will listen, nego-tiate with them on some issues, and explain the reasons behind things, they often become less argumentative. If you have a child with Oppositional Defiance Disorder (ODD) it is a lot harder to get this to work. There are a couple of book recommendations in the resources section that address parenting a child with ODD.

You might also look at diet. A friend of ours had a doctor who recommended removing high fructose corn syrup from her child's diet, and it completely turned her child's ODD behavior around. There may be a food sensitivity of some kind that is making your child feel uncomfortable, hyperactive, or on an emotional hair trigger. Removing that source of upset can make things smoother for everyone. My brother was very sensitive to a particular red food dye that was used in the 1970s, and removing that from the family's diet helped calm him down a lot as a child.

It can also help to have practice arguments, in which you pick a subject that isn't a hot topic and might even be ridiculous, and have an argument about it, getting as silly as you can. "Macaroni is eighty times better than linguini, because ants can slide inside it." "No, linguini is better because ants can slide on top, plus you can use it to tie up marauding teddy bears." This can relieve tension and sometimes make it easier to segue into issues that are setting off real arguments. Make sure all parties are in on the joke, though.

I have found attitude makes a huge difference in how well our days go. And by attitude I mean *my* attitude. When I get frustrated and grouchy everyone finds a way to disappear or to resist me. If I try to be the mean mom and force the kids to get their stuff done, it never goes well. I put on my annoyed face and say, "I've been asking you guys all day to get this table cleared off, get to it!" Then they huff, roll their eyes, put it off, take one item upstairs and never come back down, or else they cry because they already worked *so hard* putting a few small things away. If I'm too tired to get stuff done, so are they.

If I feel (and act) as though we are a team working together to keep the house clean, the family fed, and learning fun, we all do pretty well together. If I say something like, "Let's get the activity table cleared off so we can play games and have room to work on your project," suddenly everyone is pitching in and it gets done in a few minutes. Or, "We're having your friends over this afternoon, let's get the house looking nice." "If you'd like to spend a lot of uninterrupted time on your project, how about we get everything else out of the way so you can concentrate on it." This generally works, but not every time.

On a side note, our second son left the bathroom floor unimpressively swept when it was his job to clean it. When I mentioned that he needed to go over it again, he disagreed. He thought it looked fine. I chalked it up to him willfully ignoring the dirt, but guess what? He needed new glasses. In fact, my two older boys both needed their prescriptions strengthened. When we got home from getting their new glasses, I asked them to look at the floor, and suddenly they could see what I was talking about. They don't always do the most thorough job, but at least I know they can see the floor clearly now.

Attitude is doubly important when it comes to learning. Learning doesn't happen well if coercion of any kind is applied, and when learning doesn't happen it looks like they just need to buckle down and work harder, and it becomes a vicious cycle. Learning happens best with students who are self-motivated, and especially when they are pursuing knowledge for their own purposes. For example, take the attitude change our middle son had around learning math. If I had continued to force him to memorize multiplication tables without sitting down and talking to him, it's likely he would still resist doing math, and he certainly wouldn't have learned to enjoy it. There is a subtle but huge difference between, "You can't play outside until you do your multiplication tables" and, "Do you want to get these multiplication tables out of the way so there's more time to play outside? Where are you stuck?" I recommend reading *Free to Learn* by Peter Gray on the subject of self-motivated learning.

Rewards are coercion as much as punishments are. It's fine to reward your kid occasionally for a job well done; praise is a good thing when it's well deserved. Praise of effort, though, is much more effective than praise of the end result. One thing that sticks in my mind from the Early Childhood Family Education (ECFE) class that we took when the boys were young is that the ratio of remarks should be around four positive remarks to every negative one. If you weren't raised in a household where that style of feedback was the norm, it is very hard to change from a pattern of criticism to one of positivity, but it's certainly worth the effort. Try remarking on small things more frequently, with a focus on the positive, and before you say something, imagine that your spouse or a friend is saying it to you, and phrase it the way you'd like to hear it spoken to you. "It's so nice to see you and your sister having such a good time together playing that game." "You worked really hard on that project—great concentration." "Thanks for mowing the lawn. Can I get you some lemonade?" Try thanking your kids more for their help around the house and criticizing their lack of effort less, and you may well see arguments start to taper off. They'll probably never be gone completely, but life might get easier.

A few words about the damaging effect of using rewards

– Vivek Patel, meaningfulideas.com

"Rewards tend to backfire relatively quickly. They do seem like great motivators at first because we're using something our kids like to get them on board. The problem comes when kids realize (consciously or unconsciously) that we're using them to get them to do things that they don't want to do. It feels manipulative. As soon as that feeling creeps in the motivation is lost because the need for autonomy is so strong.

"Another thing about rewards is they focus on a selfish source for cooperation. We clean because we're going to get something instead of cleaning because we have learned to value the family community. It will be more effective in the long term to instill the feelings and attitudes that give rise to cooperation. Trying to force a habit pattern from the outside in will eventually create resistance and resentment.

"The third thing is that rewards diminish connection between parents and children in a very similar way that punishments do. It's hard to see that at first. In fact when I first heard this idea I totally balked at it! It seemed ridiculous to me until I gave it some serious thought. Once I realized how alike are the effect of punishment and rewards, I had to change my parenting style.

"The reason rewards damage the connection between parent and child is that it's based on conditional love and acceptance. We are in essence sending them the message that they are more worthy of our love and acceptance when they act like this and less worthy of it when they act like that.

"When our kids don't do what we want them to and we deny them the reward, it's emotionally exactly the same as taking away a privilege or sending them to their room. It's a way of saying - because you didn't live up to my expectations I'm going to use the power I have to make you less happy.

"This is why the longer and deeper route of communication, collaboration, cooperation and connection is always more effective. (It) requires a lot more patience and self-regulation too.

"When we abandon rewards and punishments and focus on engaging in a deep learning process with our kids we give them the message that we love them unconditionally no matter what they do. We teach them that mistakes are opportunities for learning and growth. They are to be embraced rather than avoided. We inspire them to know that they are fundamentally worthy of love and acceptance. This sense of unshakable self-esteem is one of the greatest gifts we can give our children as we send them out into the world."

TIP: Many homeschoolers find that when the stressors associated with school are removed the arguments decrease dramatically. If that's not the case, consider trying a more respectful parenting style.

What if my kids argue with each other all the time?

"The strong family relationships that homeschooling facilitates make it easier for all family members to enjoy being around each other."
– RACHEL GATHERCOLE, *THE WELL ADJUSTED CHILD*

Homeschoolers often get along better with their siblings than school kids do, and their relationships often improve after beginning homeschooling and spending more time with each other. One of the biggest benefits I have found with homeschooling is that our kids get along with one another remarkably well. Last summer our middle boy had a chance to spend a week having special time with his grandparents, and he chose to have his older brother accompany him. They get along much better than my brother and I did at that age, and for that I am very thankful. This is not an unusual phenomenon in homeschooling families, for several reasons.

Schoolchildren spend the best hours of the day in an institution that separates them by age and that fosters competition. Then they come home tired and hungry and have to deal with the inevitable familial friction. Not only are the siblings worn out by the end of the day, but the parents are also tired and are trying to get a number of things done. There is homework to manage and dinner to get on the table and all the things that need to happen to make the next day run smoothly. There is less time (and patience) to work through sibling conflicts, and everyone is generally crankier.

Homeschoolers, on the other hand, learn to work together earlier in the day when they are fresh and able to exhibit more patience and tolerance. They also can spend more time fostering connections with each other because they spend more time together in general. All this goes for the parents as well, who are usually less frazzled when dealing with interactions and conflict resolution during the day and have more time to build relationships between family members. Chores can be done throughout the day rather than crammed in after school or work. Then when everyone is tired out, it's easier to take a break from together time and still keep that connection.

Another advantage homeschoolers have is that their groups of friends tend to be much less age-segregated. In many cases siblings will have some of the same friends and will all play well together in a group, instead of having the younger ones written off by the older ones as pestering annoyances. It doesn't always work that way, but for the most part frequent bickering is the exception rather than the rule. That doesn't mean that each child won't have his or her own circle of friends and interests and want time away from the family to pursue them, but it does contribute to siblings getting along better. Our middle boy and our youngest don't get along with each other quite as well as they do with our oldest, who gets along great with both of them, but they do play together and have fun, and they are learning a lot about relationships. An excellent book to help foster good relations between siblings is *Siblings Without Rivalry* by Adele Faber and Elaine Mazlish. Here are a couple of ideas that I've found useful from that book.

- Feelings and actions are different. It's okay to have feelings and to express them, just don't let siblings hurt each other. We need to teach kids how to express anger and other strong feelings without doing damage.
- Kids feel that if you love them the same as everyone else it's not enough. They need to be loved uniquely, for their own selves, and appreciated for their special characteristics.

TIP: Having more time with you and with each other, and having more time when you are all fresh and cheerful, will help your kids to build better relationships with each other.

Resources and References

aspergerexperts.com - Advice for parents from people who have grown up with Asperger's

healthychildren.org - American Academy of Pediatrics site for families

healthychildren.org/English/family-life/Media/Pages/Tips-for-Parents-Digital-Age.aspx - Kids & Tech Tips for Parents

healthychildren.org/English/family-life/Media/Pages/How-to-Make-a-Family-Media-Use-Plan.aspx - How to Make a Family Media Use Plan

99 Questions and Answers about Unschooling, Kytka Hilmar-Jezek, Distinct Press (July 17, 2015)

Bedtime Math: A Fun Excuse to Stay Up Late (Bedtime Math Series), Laura Overdeck and Jim Paillot, Feiwel & Friends, 1st Edition (June 25, 2013) Ages 3-8 years

The Defiant Child: A Parent's Guide to Oppositional Defiant Disorder, Dr. Douglas A. Riley, Taylor Trade Publishing, 1st Edition (October 1, 1997)

Euler: The Master of Us All, William Dunham, Dolciani Mathematical Expositions (Book 22), American Mathematical Society (January 1, 1999)

Free to Learn: Why Unleashing the Instinct to Play Will Make Our Children Happier, More Self-Reliant, and Better Students for Life, Peter Gray, Basic Books, 1st Edition (February 10, 2015)

Free Range Learning: How Homeschooling Changes Everything, Laura Grace Weldon, Hohm Press (June 1, 2010)

Guerilla Learning: How to Give Your Kids a Real Education With or Without School, Grace Llewellyn and Amy Silver, Wiley, 1st Edition (August 1, 2001)

Here's Looking at Euclid: From Counting Ants to Games of Chance - An Awe-Inspiring Journey Through the World of Numbers, Alex Bellos, Free Press, Reprint Edition (April 19, 2011)

How Math Works, Carol Vorderman, Readers Digest (August 6, 1996)

How to Talk so Kids Will Listen, Adele Faber & Elaine Mazlish, Scribner, Updated Edition (February 7, 2012)

How to Talk So Teens Will Listen and Listen So Teens Will Talk, Adele Faber & Elaine Mazlish, William Morrow Paperbacks, Reprint Edition (August 22, 2006)

The I Hate Mathematics! Book, Marilyn Burns, Little, Brown Books for Young Readers, 1st Edition (July 30, 1975)

Kid Cooperation: How to Stop Yelling, Nagging, and Pleading and Get Kids to Cooperate, Elizabeth Pantley, New Harbinger Publications, 1st Edition (April 1, 1996)

Learning All the Time, John Holt, Da Capo Press, Revised Edition (January 22, 1990)

How Children Learn, John Holt, Da Capo Press, Revised Edition (September 4, 1995)

Teach Your Own, John Holt, Da Capo Press,; First Paperback Edition (April 2003)

Math Curse, Jon Scieszca and Lane Smith, Viking, Library Binding Edition (October 1, 1995) 3-7 years

The Number Devil: A Mathematical Adventure, Hans Magnus Enzensberger, Rotraut Susanne Berner & Michael Henry Helm, Picador (August 18, 2010) (For 11-15-year-olds, but my kids loved it starting around age 7)

Playful Parenting: An Exciting New Approach to Raising Children That Will Help You Nurture Close Connections, Solve Behavior Problems, and Encourage Confidence, Lawrence J. Cohen, Ballantine Books, Reprint Edition (April 30, 2002)

Rise Up and Salute the Sun: The Writings of Suzy Kassem, Suzy Kassem, Awakened Press, 1st Edition (May 15, 2011)

Siblings without Rivalry: How to Help Your Children Live Together So You Can Live Too, Adele Faber & Elaine Mazlish, W. W. Norton & Company, 1st Edition (April 9, 2012)

Unconditional Parenting: Moving from Rewards and Punishments to Love and Reason, Alfie Kohn, Atria Books, 1st Edition (March 28, 2006)

The Unschooling Handbook: How to Use the Whole World As Your Child's Classroom, Three Rivers Press, 2nd Edition (April 29, 1998)

Why *Do They Act That Way?* David Walsh, Ph.D., Free Press/Simon & Schuster Inc. (2004)

A few more items

How do I find time for me and my spouse?

"When he worked, he really worked. But when he played, he really PLAYED."

– DR. SEUSS (THEODORE GEISEL)

Taking care of yourself and your other relationships are as important as helping your kids grow into great people. First and foremost, make sure that your kids know that although they are very important to you, so is your partner, not to mention your own mental health. It helps if you can start when they are young, hiring a regular babysitter so they can see you taking time away from them to have some grownup fun. If you didn't manage that, and now they are throwing fits whenever you leave the house, you might have to start by scheduling something fun (and outside the house) for them. Drop them off at grandma's or for a playdate at a friend's house, and use that time to do something for yourself. As they get used to it, they will become better able to let you go out without a fuss, and eventually they will be old enough to not need a babysitter.

What kinds of things did you and your partner enjoy together when you were first dating? Do some of those things again. Visit a museum together, attend a sporting event, or go rock climbing or rollerblading. Dinner and a movie doesn't always work when younger kids still rely on mom and dad for their bedtime routine, but brunch and a movie can be just as much fun. Plus you'll be less tired. On that note, maybe you'd just like to check in to a nice hotel occasionally for a spousal date, so that you can have some uninterrupted time with nobody else but your partner. Find a few fun date options, figure out what works best in your situation, and then make sure to schedule it in. Otherwise it might not ever happen.

You can also have a date night in, rather than going out. You will need to find something to occupy the kids, and be clear with them that this is special time that shouldn't be interrupted. Try setting them up with a good children's movie or hiring a babysitter to take them to the park so you can have some together time. If you wait until they all go to bed before having a date, you might both be too tired to enjoy it. Again, make sure to have specific plans and schedule them in. Otherwise, "Let's do something Saturday" can easily turn into, "Where did Saturday go?" Yes, I know that from experience.

A friend of mine gave me some great advice when I was getting married: Schedule a weekly lunch and sex date with your spouse for times when nobody else is home. That's a lot harder to do when you don't send the kids to school. On the other hand, co-ops and playgroups can work for this if you find ones with rotating parenting responsibilities that allow everyone to have some time off. Even finding one other family to trade drop-off playdates can work.

Date night in was great for us when we just had one baby. Our boy would go down for the night at 6:00 p.m., and my husband and I would make dinner together, have a glass of wine, and relax. It wasn't so awesome when we had two small kids and my husband was working 80 hours a week. He always made a point of coming home for dinner and doing bedtimes with the kids before pulling out his laptop and grading some more, but one-on-one time was sporadic at best and usually we were both exhausted. He always made sure I had a couple of hours on Saturday mornings when I had time to myself, which was great, but in retrospect we should have made more of an effort to find a babysitter and take time for the two of us. When the boys were elementary age we had a wonderful set of babysitters, twin brothers who were up for the challenge of a toddler and two very active boys, but eventually they went off to college, and our weekend lunch dates became more infrequent.

Nowadays we generally go for a walk together first thing in the morning, getting our exercise and a chance to talk at the same time. The boys are old enough to watch out for one another and occupy themselves for a little while, and we can even go out for a weekend lunch date without worrying about them. Our problem is managing a real date on a more regular basis, as opposed to occasionally. My husband has a special outing with each boy one Sunday a month and a Lego design group one Sunday a month. Any month with a fifth Sunday is an outing day for the two of us, but that's only four times a year on average. One of my friends has a regular Saturday morning coffeeshop date with her husband, which I find charming, and we may add something like that to our routine.

What about time for yourself? Look at your day and figure out when you are most productive and when you most need a break from the kids. Then make sure you get time to both do something you love to do and also take some downtime for yourself. Because it's important! It's okay to hire a babysitter or mother's helper or ask a relative to help if it means keeping your sanity. I have been known to hire the neighbor girl to play with the kids or help organize our basement when it gets too cluttered, usually in the summer when she's not in school.

In general I am most productive in the morning. Often if something doesn't get started by about 10:00 a.m. then it doesn't get done at all. I am an early to bed, early to rise gal, and I have written this book almost completely in the early dawn hours before anyone else is up. I like to write out our tasks for the day as soon as the boys are on the computer for their first turns, and get started on chores that don't require managing the boys. That means I've started my day doing something for myself, plus worked on making the day easier. By mid afternoon I am ready for a break, and often I read and have a cup of tea while the boys have their second computer turn. I consider our homeschool social events to be breaks of a different kind, because the boys are occupied with their activities and I can catch up with some of my friends. It's also important to take time for lunch or outings with friends on a regular basis; I have a lovely group of ladies I meet with monthly for dessert and support. When my husband is home during the day, he generally takes his much-needed introvert time by having his coffee outside on the back porch in the morning, and then taking an hour or two in the afternoon to work on his Legos, do woodworking, or run errands. He finds doing things like grocery shopping to be relaxing after hanging out in a house full of energetic boys.

Different families have different ways to carve out downtime and date time. Some families have reading time, in which everyone hangs out quietly reading books or listening to an audiobook in the car. Some parents like to spend their downtime learning languages, sewing, crafting, walking the dog, exercising, or exploring social media. We have some friends who love to cook together, and spending time in the kitchen preparing dinner almost every night serves as their date time. Other friends are big gamers, and Friday nights are game nights. They have people over or go out to play board games at friends' houses. The kids now are old enough to join in instead of watching movies or playing, but that also means they are old enough to stay home when their parents go out on a date. Some people prefer to send the kids to bed early and stay up watching movies together.

It doesn't really matter if the way you manage downtime and date time doesn't look like the standard notions of a bubble bath and dinner out; what matters is that you take the time, and that you choose something that renews you and builds your relationship.

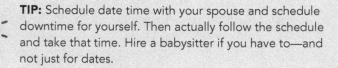

TIP: Schedule date time with your spouse and schedule downtime for yourself. Then actually follow the schedule and take that time. Hire a babysitter if you have to—and not just for dates.

What if homeschooling isn't working?

"Freedom is not worth having if it does not include the freedom to make mistakes."

− MAHATMA GANDHI

"Have no fear of perfection—you'll never reach it."

− SALVADOR DALI

If there is too much stress in your homeschooling, or it just doesn't seem to be working for you, change those things that aren't working, or change your expectations of what "working" looks like. What does it mean to you to have something work? Frequently I have found that when something felt like it wasn't working it was because I expected it to go a certain way and it wasn't happening quite like that. If I can be cognizant of my own expectations, I can see where they work and where they don't. Being present to my own expectations and how they might clash with what the boys actually need helps me stay flexible. At first I had visions of us all sitting around a clean dining room table studying together to learn as a family, surrounded by educational posters. That's not what our homeschooling has ended up looking like. Our table is often covered with the boys' creative projects that end up tidied into a pile for mealtimes, while the boys do their workbooks one on one with me upstairs sitting on my bed. We crowd in around the computer to watch educational videos, while making ourselves comfortable on various chairs and yoga balls. I read out loud to them in the evenings on the couch; we even ended up buying a couch that is a bit too large for our small living room so that all of us could cuddle together and read. The educational posters are stuck on the basement and bathroom walls. As for our version of sitting around the table together working? That comes when we take our weekly trip to the neighborhood coffee shop for ice cream and goal planning.

My boys have been very clear with me when I was attempting to make them do or learn something in a way that wasn't working. The more choice I have given them with regard to what to learn and how to learn it, the better it has gone. They have come to trust that I won't force them to keep doing something they dislike unless there is a very good reason for it (like keeping the house clean for health reasons). Keep an eye out for where things aren't going smoothly, and be mindful of the emotional health of your family. Don't wait until something is broken before you address it.

No other family is exactly like yours, so don't expect things to work exactly the same way. You might expect all your homeschooling days to look like someone else's best days, and feel you are failing when you have bad days. Not so! *Everyone* has bad days. It may even be harder for homeschoolers to talk about the bad days because nobody wants to hear the predictable response: "Just put them in school, that will solve your problems!" When parents complain about how things aren't going well at school, usually nobody leaps in to ask why they haven't started homeschooling already, but if a homeschooler complains, just about everyone who isn't another homeschooler suggests dealing with the issue by sending the kids to school. Homeschool parents generally are very selective with whom they share their parenting fail moments. Finding a group of veteran homeschoolers to commiserate with and give you ideas can be extremely beneficial, and if you can't find a local group that suits you then find an online community—the sooner the better.

What if it isn't working at all? Again, change it! Sometimes what worked for a while will no longer fit as your family grows and matures. Sometimes you have an idea of how you want homeschooling to be for your family and that's not how it's going. Sometimes it seems like nobody is doing what they are supposed to do and everybody is fighting. Take a break, step back, and really think about what it would take to get to a situation that serves your family best. What do you want for them? What do you want for yourself? What does your family want? Get together and talk about which goals to set, why they are important, and how best to reach them. There are lots of different ways to achieve educational excellence and family harmony, and that will look different for every family. Maybe you need to work with a specialist, or focus more on art than on academics for a while, or try a few select classes. Maybe taking a vacation is in order, or giving the kids more autonomy over their education. Be as receptive and creative as necessary. When it seems like homeschooling isn't working, the best thing to do is pause and focus on rebuilding family bonds. After you have a good rapport with one another is the time to address changes that might need to be made.

I go through this process with my family on a regular basis. For example, the older two were having three half-hour computer turns a day, but they ended up watching each other's turns for a total of three hours each. It felt like we had very little time between turns to get chores and learning and physical activity and social activities done. They were rushed, I was frazzled, and it didn't look at all like how I envisioned our homeschool learning experience. In a quiet moment when we were all happy and relaxed, I talked to them about how rushed and stressful our days seemed, and how the days often revolved around the computer. I asked them for ideas on how we could make our homeschool day more enjoyable, and together we decided to change the computer turns to 30-minute sessions twice daily, and have them share the watching only in the afternoon. That gives us a much bigger chunk of time in the middle of the day, which we all like much better. We still do educational work on the computer, which is separate from game time, and setting them up with a specific amount of time to work on coding and typing and watching educational videos was a good compromise when reducing the free play time.

One thing to keep in mind is that there may not be one solution that is great for everyone in the family. What works for one child may not work for another. Our three boys are so different from one another. Our oldest enjoys challenging himself, and he loves taking things like math and language classes and chemistry labs. Our middle boy would much rather figure things out himself through reading books, watching how-to videos, and doing hands-on experiments. Academic classes do not interest him at all, and I find he actively resists anything that seems like "teaching" to him. Our youngest is interested in learning about and making complex things with gears and tools. What excites one is sometimes fun for everyone, but just as often it isn't.

Together with your family, look at different approaches to learning itself as well as different subjects to figure out what will be most supportive of each individual. I discuss various learning styles in chapter 5, which may be helpful. Find out what is the best way for each person to learn, and help them find resources that cater to that. At the same time help them develop other learning styles. Besides learning styles, there are various environments you can experiment with to find what is most effective. Some people take online classes, some prefer to learn individually or with small groups of like-minded students, some attend weekly co-ops. I know plenty of families who took one child out of school to homeschool while the other children stayed in school, where they thrived. I also know plenty of families who sent one or more of their children to school after exclusively homeschooling up to that point. If what you're doing doesn't feel right, explore other options. Just do it from a place of mindfulness, love, and encouragement, rather than frustration or punishment, when making a change.

Mission Statement Template

Our purpose as a family is to ...
We will accomplish this by:
- living by our main principles of ... and ...
- making our home a place of ... and ...
- prioritizing ...
- treating each other ...

One tool a lot of families use to keep them on track is a Family Mission Statement. This involves a family sitting down to talk about their values and principles, and coming up with a statement that describes how they intend to accomplish their purpose. Some people find this very helpful, and they read it together at the start of every day. It can help to keep you and your family going in the right direction, inspired by the possibilities. It can give you a boost when you're in a rut, and remind you of why you chose to homeschool in the first place. It should be short and sweet, just a few sentences about what your family stands for, and it should be meaningful to you. The Franklin Covey website has a page that will walk you through creating a mission statement if you would like guidance.

Instead of a mission statement, I have done a homeschool goals list that I go over briefly on Mondays when we are discussing what we want to work on that week. That helps me keep my perspective when things aren't going well, to remind me that finishing a particular workbook or program is not the be-all, end-all of education. It also helps to broaden my children's ideas about what they want to work on to help them become better people. Our goals list has slowly evolved through time as we grow, and writing it down here has actually helped me hone the wording of it. Yes, even a mission statement or goals list can stop working for your family. Update it as needed, and keep referring to it. Nothing is going to go smoothly all the time; having a broader vision of your goals helps keep you on track even when you need to change the day-to-day implementation.

Our Homeschool Goals

- Learn to learn, and to find the resources we need for that learning
- Ask for what we need to succeed, and advocate for ourselves
- Cultivate friendships and family relationships
- Contribute to the family and to our community and to the world
- Discover what we love and pursue excellence in those areas
- Invest in our future through education and good money management
- Strive to be kind, brave, happy, and healthy

TIP: Nothing is set in stone. Your family will grow and mature, and you should be prepared to change how you are working together several times over the years, keeping an end goal in sight.

Can I keep homeschooling through high school?

"A homeschool parent's job is not to have everything to teach, but to put everything within reach."
– JEANNE FAULCONER, THEHOMESCHOOLMOM.COM

There are two points in the homeschooling cycle that tend to stress parents out the most: when they are first starting out and when their kids are beginning high school. And no, it's not because it's impossibly hard to do. First, it's because people keep asking in a worried tone, "Are you going to keep homeschooling through high school?" You can't get away from people questioning your ability to homeschool through high school. And this can raise doubts about your competency and capability, and thus raise your anxiety level. It's easy to start questioning yourself and worrying that it can't be done, even if you have been planning on it. Second, there are plenty of things about high school that need managing. Classes at a high-school level are generally what's needed to get into college, so you have to find a way to provide those for your kids. You have to do transcripts for those classes, and make sure all the subjects are covered. Also, high-school teachers specialize. Nobody teaches all the subjects anymore, therefore expecting a homeschool parent to teach all the subjects strikes many people as unreasonable, not to mention impossible.

Fortunately, you don't have to become an expert in every subject you teach. You just have to become an expert on finding resources that will help your kids learn what they need to know. And getting into college doesn't mean having a transcript that is in all ways identical to a school transcript. In fact, colleges often look for students who are different from all the rest, especially those students who are self-motivated. There are plenty of sample transcripts out there for homeschoolers that aren't difficult to fill out. Many colleges even accept portfolios of work from homeschoolers in place of a traditional transcript. Just make sure you keep good records of the work they have done; trying to reconstruct coursework from memory isn't recommended. And there are plenty of teaching options for the high-school years, just as there are for the preschool and grade-school years.

Homeschoolers benefit from having a huge amount of flexibility in their learning options. I am going to list a few here to give you some ideas to get you started. Courses might include online high-school classes such as Khan Academy (and many more), online college classes like the Massive Open Online Courses (MOOCs) offered either directly through universities or through platforms such as EdX and Coursera, and other independent online study. Courses might be more traditional, using a specific homeschool curriculum or distance-learning programs, or taking classes from local schools, including homeschool co-ops, high schools, and community colleges. Some states have a Post-Secondary Enrollment Option (PSEO) that allows students to take university classes while still in high school. Then there are things like private tutoring, mentoring, or trading expertise with other homeschool parents. Also, be on the lookout for less obvious ideas such as apprenticeships, internships, vocational training opportunities, independent studies, volunteering, museum and community center programs, exchange student/study abroad programs, language-immersion programs, and independent travel. There are a few programs out there for homeschool travel, so that the class trip abroad is not something you have to sacrifice if you homeschool.

What about electives? I could write a whole chapter just listing all the homeschool electives that I know about. No matter how great a conventional school may be, they just don't have the resources to offer as many electives as homeschoolers have to choose from. Just off the top of my head, I know local homeschoolers who have taken classes in ballroom dance, Irish dance, martial arts, fencing, print-making and book binding, ceramics, theater and stage management, play and scriptwriting, filmmaking, photography, drawing, sculpture, woodworking, metalworking, blacksmithing, board game design, video game programming, podcasting, bike repair, choir, orchestra,

Japanese, Spanish, French, cooking, sewing, knitting, and more.

Obviously, being in a metropolitan area broadens your options for in-person classes, but don't let being in a rural area limit your thinking. Besides the obvious solution of online classes, ask around. Most people have a wide variety of skills, and you never know who might be able to lead a class in French or art or fencing until you ask. I never knew my mom fenced until our oldest started his fencing classes and she was excited to hear about it. If you can't find enough homeschoolers to fill a class, open it up to others in your community. You'll build your organizing skills and find new friends all at the same time. As your kids get older, have them help with organizing things like classes and talent shows and science fairs. Initiative is a great skill to showcase on a college application.

Many people worry needlessly about diplomas when homeschooling through the high school years. Most colleges, universities, and workplaces will accept a homeschool diploma, and it does not have to be accredited. Plenty of public and private schools are not accredited, and they still issue valid diplomas. The most common way to obtain a homeschool diploma is for the person in charge of the student's education to issue one. That is, either download a template and fill it out yourself or use a company such as HomeschoolDiploma.com to print one out. Then sign it. Some people also recommend having the signature notarized to look more official.

A homeschool diploma should include:
- The name of the institution (your homeschool name) issuing the diploma
- The full name of the student
- A statement that the student has completed the requirements for a high school diploma
- The city and state where the diploma is issued
- The date the diploma is issued
- The educator's signature

There are other ways to obtain a diploma. If your student is taking classes through an umbrella school or correspondence program, or through an online public school or virtual charter school, those institutions will often be the ones to grant the diploma. Occasionally, states allow or require homeschooled students to obtain their diplomas through a local public high school or other sanctioned institution or association, so make sure you check your state's laws. It is also possible to take the General Educational Development (GED) exam as an alternative, but be aware that people may assume a GED means the student was unable to complete the class requirements. Have them do the work you think they need so they can receive a diploma, if possible.

Homeschooling through high school isn't really the impossible feat that many people seem to think it is. Use it as a time to help your kids develop their reasoning skills, hone their study techniques, and explore all the interesting subjects they have time for. Make sure there is also time for family and friends, and for other those things your family prioritizes, such as travel, volunteering, and exercise. Most of all, have fun, and enjoy the time you have together.

TIP: You don't have to know every high school subject well enough to teach it. You just need to help your kids find the resources to learn what they need to know, and keep good records.

But won't they miss prom?

"My definition of a free society is a society where it is safe to be unpopular."
– ADLAI E STEVENSON II

Don't worry, homeschoolers don't have to miss out on prom! Here in the Twin Cities, there are homeschoolers who put on proms for their kids, and kids who organize their own proms. There's nothing stopping you from doing the same. Or you could look into having your kids attend the local school's prom if that's what appeals to them. When I was in school I went to a couple of proms where neither I nor my date actually attended the school holding it. These days it's not so easy to crash a school dance, and may require you as principal to sign forms for your student. Going to someone else's prom, though, may be inferior to homeschoolers creating their own. In my experience, prom was fabulous for those who were popular, and it was great training in leadership and event planning for them. They got to plan it, promote it, decorate for it, choose music or a band for it, and then enjoy it with their other popular friends. Everybody else either came along for a good time with their dates, came along defiantly without dates, came along and felt awkward with someone who was only technically a "date," or stayed home and felt bad about not having any date at all. It's my understanding that more school proms these days are accepting of people coming as groups of friends without dates, and that certainly was the case in the less formal "dances" that were organized at my school.

TOM SAYS: *I fell into another category than those listed above—those who found the whole idea of prom to be ridiculous and ignored it altogether.*

The homeschoolers I've seen tend to be very inclusive, organizing events where everyone is welcome, with or without a date, and their outfits tend to be much more original and fun than the traditional prom attire. Plus, a higher percentage of attendees generally gets experience in planning and coordinating the events, since it's a much smaller group. For a lot of homeschooled kids, though, prom isn't the huge deal it's made out to be in conventional school. They can dress up and go out for dinner and dancing with friends on their own schedule. Prom is only a big deal when everyone around you thinks it's a big deal, otherwise it's just another chance to dress up and have fun in your already busy and interesting life.

TIP: Help your kids organize their own prom, find a local homeschool group that puts on a prom, go to a local school prom, or just organize more formal group social dates like a fancy dinner and dancing. Hire a limousine if you really want to!

Will they be able to get into a good college?

"Some people get an education without going to college. The rest get it after they get out."

– MARK TWAIN

More and more colleges are accepting homeschoolers, who tend to make very good students. Why would homeschoolers in particular make good students? College is a time when young people are gaining independence from their parents and learning to be responsible for themselves, and they are often as interested (if not more so) in exploring their freedom as they are their education. Many homeschoolers have already been given responsibility for their education and so are highly motivated to get as much as possible out of their courses. Homeschoolers also are used to interacting with adults as individuals rather than as students to teachers, and they are generally at ease around their professors and with applying themselves to the subject at hand. "I…announced to my wife that the best student in my college composition class had been home-schooled," wrote David McGrath in his *Chicago Tribune* article about his experience with homeschooled college students and how it changed his view of homeschooling. Also check out the Journal of College Admission's fall 2004 issue for more insights and studies on how homeschoolers do in college.

It's not just a few colleges here and there that accept home-schooled students. A quick Google search for college and home-schoolers brought up a page from 2013 that listed one thousand well-regarded colleges in the U.S. already known for accepting home-schoolers. It is quite possible to find one, if not several, that suit your college-bound homeschooler's best interests. Take your time, look at all the options, and visit campuses to get a feel for the best fit.

Often admissions offices will provide a guide for homeschoolers that details which tests they need to take and what paperwork they should provide; colleges have different requirements, so plan ahead.

You might want to call the admissions offices of those colleges your student is most interested in; sometimes the online requirements don't tell the whole story about what they are looking for. OnlineCollege.org provides a good general guide for homeschoolers applying to college, and HomeschoolSuccess.com has a lot of detailed information about the whole process. Students will need to have documentation of all coursework, take the correct tests for the colleges in question, and spend time developing extracurricular skills. Many people assume that homeschoolers are indeed hermits, and need to be convinced that homeschooled applicants are used to participating with people of all ages in their communities.

Colleges, especially highly competitive ones, want to see homeschoolers' excellent classwork, high test scores, well-developed extracurricular activities, and plenty of community service. Enrolling your kids in classes at a local community college or online college courses during the high school years can help with the admissions process as well as preparing your kids for their college years.

One of my good friends from college was homeschooled until high school. She took one year of public school, which she didn't much enjoy except for the theater program. Then she approached the local community college, and they were willing to have her as long as the high school was willing to let her go. After a year at the community college she transferred to my university, where she was much happier. As a transfer student rather than an incoming freshman, she refused to tell people her age, and everyone assumed she was older rather than younger because of her maturity level. She was the first person I encountered who had been homeschooled, and she made a very good impression on me.

Now that you know homeschoolers can not only get into good colleges but are also likely to excel there, I want to poke a few holes into the assumption that going to college is the best thing for everyone. My husband and I went to a university filled with overachievers who were there to study. Even there, we saw instances of students drinking so much they needed to be taken to the emergency room.

There were date rapes. And lots of students came down with mono-nucleosis, including me and my best friends. One of those friends was hit really hard, and it turned into chronic fatigue syndrome that affected her energy levels for years and kept her from graduating. Living in dorms and eating in cafeterias can lead to illnesses spreading like wildfire, and being on their own for the first time leads some people to act irresponsibly. Unfortunately, if you're an adult the first time you're allowed to make stupid decisions, the repercussions of those decisions can last for years. On the other hand, binge drinking, assault, and illness can happen anywhere, so avoiding college doesn't mean avoiding risk. Make sure you research the atmosphere of campus life and not just the academics when looking at colleges, as the whole experience can differ radically from one to the next.

What about the financial side of college? Forty years ago a college education was reasonably affordable, and it was the most reliable way to secure a steady, well-paying job for the rest of your life. Things have changed pretty radically since then. Federal and state funding for colleges and universities has dropped steadily, and tuition has risen dramatically at most institutions. More and more students are taking on an enormous amount of debt that will be a financial drain on their lives for decades. A college degree no longer guarantees a job of any kind, much less a well-paying one. Many jobs are being outsourced to other countries, while even more are being automated. Taking on a crippling amount of debt to obtain a college degree doesn't make sense for more and more people. Fortunately, there are some affordable options, but you may have to look harder to find them, from community colleges to obscure scholarships. If large scholarships don't loom on the horizon, consider universities in countries that do have decent funding.

On the other hand, there is a shortage of people in skilled trades because so many of us have been led to believe that college and an office job is the way to go. California is now actively recruiting students for its technical schools, after years of pushing them toward college. Trade schools offer entry to service jobs that cannot be outsourced, which is a big concern these days. Not everyone is suited to a nine-to-five job—and thank goodness. Otherwise we would be sorely lacking in richness in our lives. Who would create new music or play the classics? Who would be the chefs and the artists? Who would build houses and bridges and skyscrapers? Who would do the plumbing and wiring? Who would provide care for ailing parents and injured children?

And who would start innovative companies? There are plenty of successful people who didn't graduate from college. Fairly recent companies started by people without a college degree include Drop-Box, Facebook, Tumblr, Mashable, Spotify, Pinterest, and CodeAcademy. For those not as interested in computers, look at Richard Branson, Rachael Ray, JetBlue, Whole Foods, and Wendy's.

College is not the only way to succeed, nor is it the only way to make good contacts. The way to succeed is to have a vision of what you want to achieve and the grit and determination to make it happen. The vision could be anything from a career in a particular field to traveling the world or to starting the next big company. It could be raising great kids and keeping a lovely home. It could be a career in art or welding or simultaneous translation. Success is about going after what you want, not taking a specific path. It may be that a college degree is the best path to get there, and it may not. I recommend the book *Hacking Your Education* by Dale Stephens for ideas on succeeding outside the college box. Keep your eyes open for alternate paths to success. Things may change as our boys get older, but I won't be surprised if at least one of them chooses a career that doesn't call for a college degree.

 TIP: Colleges like homeschooled students because they are often very independent, motivated and mature, and they stand out from the crowd. If college isn't the best fit, there are plenty of other options if you look for them.

Will my kids really succeed in life?

"The most effective (and least destructive) way to help a child succeed…is to do everything possible to help her fall in love with what she's doing, to pay less attention to how successful she was (or is likely to be) and show more interest in the task…Encourage more, judge less, and love always."

– ALFIE KOHN, *UNCONDITIONAL PARENTING*

Homeschooling is not a guarantee of success just as public school is not a guarantee of success, but homeschooling certainly shouldn't put your kids at a disadvantage compared to other people. In fact, quite a number of famously successful people were homeschooled. Here is a short list: Leonardo da Vinci, Ansel Adams, Charlie Chaplin, Wolfgang Amadeus Mozart, Orville and Wilbur Wright, George Washington Carver, Winston Churchill, Sandra Day O'Connor, Pearl S. Buck, Agatha Christie, Samuel Clemens (Mark Twain), Will Rogers, Booker T. Washington, Albert Schweitzer, Florence Nightingale, explorers Lewis and Clark, and ten American presidents. And in case you're looking at that list and thinking that things were different back then, here are a few more successful people who were homeschooled: Whoopi Goldberg, Michelle Kwan, Serena and Venus Williams, Justin Timberlake, Tim Tebow, Emma Watson, Christina Aguilera, and LeAnne Rimes. Homeschoolers are in good company, and not only with celebrities. I just picked out a few of the best-known names.

Your kids will succeed or fail to the extent they are motivated to succeed and have confidence that they will succeed. That has to do with *how* they were educated and nothing to do with *where* they are educated, because the *atmosphere* of the educational environment can make a difference. Motivation for success comes from the values they learn at home and in the community, about hard work and persistence and having goals to work toward and an overall life purpose. If their only goal is to finish school and get a job, that is likely what will happen. And then what? Having a purpose in life will keep them going and give them continuing goals to shoot for, even if that purpose changes and matures over time.

I discussed success more in the previous section, so I won't repeat it all here. If you're homeschooling because you want your kids to be happy, well-adjusted people who know how to be curious and follow their ideas through to the end, and if you're willing to change things up if they're not working, you're on the right path.

> **TIP:** Success in life is not guaranteed by homeschooling; neither is it guaranteed by going the conventional education route. In fact, there are no guarantees. Homeschooling gives you a very good chance to teach your kids the values that lead to success. The rest is up to them and to their innate abilities.

Resources and References

BlakeBoles.com - High school travel opportunities for homeschoolers

coursera.org - Coursera provides both free and for-credit online university classes

edx.org - EdX also provides both free and for-credit online university classes

HomeschoolDiploma.com - Templates for high school diplomas

homeschoolsuccess.com - High school planning for college admissions success

khanacademy.org - Khan Academy provides free resources from Kindergarten up

meaningfulideas.com - Vivek Patel's conscious parenting site

msb.franklincovey.com - Resource for building mission statements

onlinecollege.org - Information on college admissions for homeschoolers

TheHomeschoolMom.com - Lots of homeschooling resources, including college admissions

uncollege.org - A gap year program to help launch students into success

"8 Hugely Successful People Who Didn't Graduate College," Entrepreneur, Thomas Smale, August 19, 2015

Guerrilla Learning: How to Give Your Kids a Real Education With or Without School, Grace Llewellyn, Amy Silver, Wiley; 1st Edition (August 1, 2001)

Hacking Your Education: Ditch the Lectures, Save Tens of Thousands, and Learn More Than Your Peers Ever Will, Dale J. Stephens, TarcherPerigee (March 5, 2013)

"Homeschoolers on to College: What Research Shows Us," The Journal of College Admission, Number 185, Fall 2004, http://www.ahem.info/Documents/ JournalofCollegeAdmissionFall04.pdf

"In a Class by Themselves," Christine Foster, Stanford Alumni Magazine (November/December 2000)

"These 19 Insanely Successful College Dropouts Prove You Don't Need A Degree," Business Insider, Max Nisen & Vivian Giang, September 3, 2013

"What changed this teacher's mind about home schooling," Chicago Tribune, David McGrath, February 18, 2016

"Why we need vocational education," The Washington Post, Valerie Strauss and Mark Phillips, June 5, 2012

Some Specifics

Where do I find good resources?

Your local library is a wonderful resource. I know I discussed libraries before, but I feel like I can't talk them up enough. Join your local branch, and see if there are other libraries in your area you could join. Some library cards are good for all public libraries in a city or county. Smaller towns might require you to get a separate card for each library, but it's worth the effort. (There are phone apps that let you put all your library card bar codes in one place, so you don't have to fumble around for the right card.) Get to know your local librarians. They generally really enjoy helping others find the information they need. The librarians at our local library have been wonderful in helping us to find all kinds of interesting books, and have suggested a number of books that we otherwise wouldn't have thought of. Librarians can also teach you how to use the inter-library loan system to order books that their library might not have. Libraries have children's fiction and non-fiction books, encyclopedia sets, classic and contemporary novels, and everything from books on obscure history and science subjects to audio books and movies. Ours even has foreign language curricula, music CDs, nature backpacks, and museum passes available to check out. Many libraries now offer ebooks as well.

Libraries also can offer a number of other resources and programming. Ours has computers, printers, and copiers available for members, and offers a variety of free programs for both kids and adults. They have story time for little kids, book clubs for elementary and older kids, and book clubs for adults. There are maker workshops and science days. There are author nights and music nights and movie nights. If your library doesn't have what you need, offer to work with them to put something together. Our homeschooling neighbor loves silent films, and approached the library about doing a Charlie Chaplin movie day. Now we have the chance to watch Charlie Chaplin and Buster Keaton and more for free at the library every spring, with popcorn included. Our library also has a summer reading program in which kids can earn free books and journals by completing a certain amount of reading and activities.

As a homeschooling family, we are always on the lookout for free resources, and there are a lot out there besides just the library. Often your local pediatrician's office will post lists of activities for kids. Our occupational therapists' office has two boards where they post upcoming community activities that are free or inexpensive, and they also have handouts listing plenty of ideas for activities at home or the park. Our parks and recreation department offers free afternoon activities Monday through Thursday in the summer and on select days during the school year, free ice cream socials in the park, movies and music in the park, even fitness in the park. They offer low cost classes as well. Bookstores often have free events, including author events and parties. Both Barnes and Noble and Half Price Books offer summer reading programs that the kids can use to get free books, and Barnes and Noble has a party in the fall for kids who participated. (They also email coupons for free treats for elementary-age kids' birthdays, which can't be underestimated.) Museums often have free days, although you'll want to plan for crowds. Colleges and universities generally have reasonably priced concerts, theater showings, and sporting events, and sometimes you can even find free ones. Plus there are free lectures that anyone can attend. My university hosted talks by Jane Goodall and the Dalai Lama that were open to the public, although most speakers won't be quite so notable. Also look for free resources through places like freecycle.org and Little Free Libraries. We have gotten some great books from the neighborhood free libraries. There is also a great compendium, *Homeschool Your Child For Free*, by Gold & Zielinsky.

There are plenty of free online resources as well, some of which have a payment option in case you want to upgrade. A good place to

start is the list created by the Pearce family bloggers at <u>PearceOnEarth.</u>
<u>com</u>, which has an impressive collection of free educational sites. For
something even more comprehensive, go to A2ZHomeschooling.com.
Get on <u>clickschooling.com</u>'s email list to be sent links to free educational sites Monday through Saturday. We use YouTube a lot, especially
the channels for TedEd, Science Max, Crash Course, Minute Physics,
Minute Earth, VSauce, Brain Scoop, Physics Girl, and Veritasium. The
list goes on and on, as a little online research will show.

There are plenty of other good resources that will help you save
money, but aren't necessarily free. Many places will offer a school or
educator's discount; just remember to bring your documentation. You
can print free student and teacher ID cards that are generally acceptable
from the Homeschool Buyers Co-op website; many larger homeschool
groups also print membership cards. Some people simply use a copy of
the paperwork that they sent in to the school district. Most museums
will have special membership rates for teachers, and many bookstores
and craft stores give educator discounts as well. Make sure to check
out museums' class offerings, as well as your local parks and recreation
department and community education department. Even our zoo has
homeschool classes, as well as classes that anyone can take. The most
cost-effective way to take field trips and see performances is to ask about
group rates, school rates, and special school performances. Sometimes
you can get in with just your family, other times you will need to recruit
other homeschoolers to get a group rate. Here in the Twin Cities, my
friend Nic runs the Homeschool Adventures website, which lists classes
and performances offered to homeschoolers and serves as a platform for
homeschoolers to organize field trips and find other people to help fill
out groups. Many people use Facebook to get groups together for events
and field trips, so join some local pages and go to events.

For inexpensive books and materials, we've had very good luck
finding things at used book and resource sales put on by local homeschool groups. Bear in mind that many things specifically written for
homeschoolers are religious; look carefully at materials before spending
money on them. We also get lots of great books from thrift stores,

as well as other materials such as binders, manipulatives, and games. Games can be very educational, and buying them new can be very expensive; at two to four dollars apiece from the thrift store, we've managed to amass quite a large collection. Used materials online can be reasonably priced, too. We use Amazon.com for a lot of our used books, as well as PaperbackSwap.com. There are also groups on Facebook specifically dedicated to curriculum sales. Another great way to go is the Homeschool Buyers Co-op, where they offer group discounts on a wide selection of educational items, from books to online curricula to DVD sets to Lego kits. Educents is another educational discount site.

One great way to keep costs down and keep the house from filling up with extra stuff is to ask the grandparents for what you need as birthday and holiday gifts. My mom has bought us a museum membership every year, and she buys the boys subscriptions to magazines such as Ranger Rick, Zoobooks, Spider, and Muse. We also keep an Amazon wishlist. You can have as many wish lists as you like, keeping some private while making others public. Each of the boys has a list under my account, and throughout the year we add to it or remove items as we find things they want. Then the grandparents know what the boys actually want, and we get great books and movies and toys that help complete our educational library. In the past we have asked the boys to prioritize one book, one movie, and one toy as their top wishes, although these days the older boys generally want books and games. Between the library and Netflix we usually can find whichever movie we want to watch.

Mostly we have used the Brain Quest workbooks for elementary school. They are inexpensive, provide good explanations, and cover a lot of the basics. Our middle son was comparing the Brain Quest workbook to several other brands recently when deciding what he wanted to work on this year, and he observed that none of the others explained the math as well. The Sylvan Learning math compendium that we keep in the car was fine for practice. He prefers to figure things out on his own, with parents as backup if he's having trouble, so good explanations are a must. Sometimes, especially when we are heading off on a road trip, we'll all go to the bookstore and poke around in the educational section to see if there are smaller workbooks that look interesting to the

kids, although travel games are more likely to interest them these days.
They have enjoyed fine motor workbooks such as Mystery Mosaics,
Extreme Dot-to-Dots, and cursive workbooks. Now that they are getting older, we have bought a few curricula that they specifically asked
for, such as a geometry curriculum and a literature curriculum.

One thing we splurge on is subscription boxes. We bought the
boys subscriptions to monthly activity boxes from KiwiCo.com,
which has a range of lines to choose from. They love getting the
boxes and doing the activities, although our basement has been filling
up with the completed boxes. We put the boxes on hold during the
warmer months and reactivate the subscription when we need more
inside activities to keep us busy in winter. Another thing we have just
begun is a meal box, to help expand their cooking repertoire. When
it doesn't come from mom, sometimes it's more interesting, and the
boys have been excited to cook meals they picked out and ordered.

This list of resources makes it sound like we spend hours every
day doing workbooks, taking classes, reading literature, going on field
trips, watching educational videos, doing projects, and finding more
resources. We really don't, I promise. This list covers ten years' worth
of ideas, some of which we use all the time, some of which we use
occasionally, and others we grew out of or found didn't work well for
our family. Resources are like food. Provide a healthy and interesting balance of options, offer them regularly, and see what they like.
Keep offering, encourage trying new things, but don't force anything.
When they're ready for something, especially if it's their own idea,
kids will devour it. Otherwise they'll poke at it, whine about it, or
flat out refuse it. The more you push something, the more resistance
you will get. As you can see, there are so many options out there that
together you can always find something that will work.

TIP: There are loads of great resources out there, but
you can't do them all. Choose a few that work for your
family right now, focus on those, adjust as needed, and
let the rest go.

Learning styles and multiple intelligences

"Do not train a child to learn by force or harshness; but direct them to it by what amuses their minds, so that you may be better able to discover with accuracy the peculiar bent of the genius of each."
– PLATO

One thing you can do as a parent is help your child figure out what kind of learner they are, so that they can find the ways that work the best for them when they need to learn something. Schools cater mainly to specific kinds of learners, and those students generally do quite well in school. The rest of the students tend to struggle, not because they are less intelligent but because they need different kinds of input to learn best. We like to look at both learning styles and intelligence types, and there is some crossover between the two.

Schools are best at teaching students who enjoy learning through reading and writing, and through spoken instruction. There is not as much help for students who prefer to see pictures and diagrams, or those who need a hands-on experience to learn something, especially after around third grade. As for intelligence type, students whose dominant intelligences are linguistic and/or logical-mathematical are best served by the school system. Students with more dominant visual, musical, kinesthetic, interpersonal, intrapersonal, or naturalistic intelligences are often left out and made to feel that they fall short because they don't conform to what the system considers to be intelligence.

Fortunately, homeschoolers aren't confined to using lectures, chalkboards, and textbooks for learning. You have access to a whole world of learning, and you and your kids are the ones who get to decide what serves your kids best, not the school system. First, help your kids figure out what their learning modalities are. Once they understand which type of input helps them to learn best, they (and you) can tailor their lessons individually. Use the Learning Styles questionnaire to figure out the easiest ways you and your kids learn. I was surprised to learn that my middle son, who adores reading, actually prefers to learn things through listening and watching videos.

It's a good idea to offer information in a variety of styles, and for a variety of intelligences. The more ways something is presented, the more likely the knowledge is to stick. Also, it will help your kids develop more than one learning style, so they have more options in how to learn, and more developed intelligences, so they will be better rounded people. Usually, a person will have one dominant style or modality while still having access to the others, although that's not always the case. A friend of mine in college was primarily kinesthetic, with auditory as backup, but could never picture anything in his mind. In fact, he was stunned to learn that I see actual pictures in my head, like a photograph, and that most people can, at least to some extent. I see not just snapshots, but movies in 3D, and I was amazed to learn that he couldn't picture anything at all. He thought that when someone said, "picture this," it was metaphorical. We also have a friend with severe dyslexia who needs to listen to audiobooks to keep up in class. Reading is never going to be an optimal way for him to learn. In our family, we have several different kinds of learning styles, and when we're all learning things together we try to present the material in multiple ways. I read out loud, we watch videos, we read books on the subject, we use workbooks, and we make projects and go on field trips.

Learning Styles Questionnaire

People learn in many different ways. Four ways of getting information into the brain include Visual (pictures), Auditory (listening), Reading/Writing, and Kinesthetic (feeling). Learning through a combination of all four is considered ideal, and each person has his or her own unique combination of primary and auxiliary styles.

The following questions will help you explore your child's learning style. Write down the letter that best explains his or her preference. If a single response doesn't match, write down two or more choices. V = Visual (pictures), A = Auditory, R = Reading/Writing, K = Kinesthetic.

1. You are about to give directions to a friend. She wants to visit your house and she doesn't know how to get there. Would you:
- V - draw a map on paper?
- A - tell her the directions?
- R - write down the directions without a map?
- K - go get her and show her the way?

2. You are going to visit a friend and don't know how to get there. Would you like him to:
- V - draw you a map on paper?
- A - tell you directions on the phone?
- R - write down the directions without a map?
- K - come get you and show you the way?

3. Your friend wants to know all about a road trip your family is taking. Would you:
- A - tell her about it?
- R - make her a copy of the itinerary?
- V - show her on a globe or map?

4. You are going to cook dessert as a special treat for your family. Do you choose one by:
- A - asking for ideas from others?
- K - cooking something familiar without needing instructions?
- V - thumbing through a cookbook looking for ideas from the pictures?
- R - reading the recipes in a cookbook?

5. You are going to teach other kids all about national parks. Would you:
- K - suggest a tour of a national park?
- V - show them pictures or movies about national parks?
- R - give them books about national parks?
- A - give them a talk about national parks?

6. You are about to buy new headphones. Other than price, what would most influence your decision:
- A - a friend talking about them?
- R - reading details about them?
- K - listening to music on them?
- V - how cool they look?

7. Recall a time when you learned how to do something like playing a new board game. (Pick something that is not a physical skill like riding a bike.) How did you learn best? By:
- V - visual clues like pictures, diagrams and charts?
- R - written instructions?
- A - listening to somebody explaining it?
- K - doing it?

8. Which of these games do you prefer?
- V - Pictionary
- R - Scrabble
- K - Charades
- A - Twenty Questions

9. You are about to learn to use a new program or game on a computer. Would you:
- V - ask someone to show you?
- K - ask someone to help you do it?
- R - read the manual or instructions?
- A - ask someone to tell you about it?

10. You are not sure whether a word should be spelled "dependent" or "dependant." Do you:
- R - look it up in the dictionary?
- V - see the word in your mind and choose the best way it looks?
- A - sound it out?
- K&V - write both versions down to see which one looks best?

11. Apart from price, what would most influence your decision to buy

a particular book?
- K - using a friend's copy
- A - a friend talking about it
- R - skimming parts of it
- V - the pictures

12. A new movie is out. What would most influence your decision to go see it or not?
- A - your friends liked it
- R - you read a review of it
- V - you saw a preview of it

13. Do you prefer to learn from:
- R - books, textbooks, articles, information sheets?
- K - field trips, labs, hands-on sessions?
- V - flow charts, diagrams, pictures, slides, videos?
- A - lectures, discussions, guest speakers, talks?

Adapted from Fleming, N.D. and Mills, C. (1992) "Not another inventory, rather a catalyst for reflections," in *To Improve the Academy*, vol. 11: 137-155

After figuring out your kids' best learning styles, find their dominant intelligences by using Howard Gardner's *Multiple Intelligences*. Help them develop their strengths, make sure they know that they are intelligent in their own ways, and work with them on their less dominant areas. At the very least, expose them to all the different kinds of intelligences. You never know which strengths they might develop, and it will give them a better understanding of people with different intelligences. We certainly had no idea that our oldest would turn out to be highly musical, we just wanted to expose the kids to music to give them the experience. Our middle son is really starting to enjoy piano, too, now that he's learned to read music more fluently. I suspect that my husband has musical intelligence, as well, he just never had a chance to develop it.

Gardner's multiple intelligences that he describes generally complement the learning styles above. An intelligence is different from a learning style. Style is how an individual approaches materials whereas intelligence is their computational power in a particular area. I have found both to be useful in working with my kids, which is why I have included both here. Gardner, on the other hand, feels that labeling students with "learning styles" is unhelpful and unscientific. I have given some learning style suggestions following the sidebar for each of his intelligences.

Summary of Howard Gardner's Multiple Intelligences Theory

In Howard Gardner's theory, developed in 1983, he describes eight separate types of intelligence. Several types of intelligence can be present in a single individual. A strength or weakness in one intelligence does not predict a strength or weakness in any of the other intelligences. Just as there are multiple intelligences, there are also multiple ways to learn and understand something. Gardner now believes there may be 10 or more intelligences.

Linguistic Intelligence (Word Smart)

Children whose linguistic or verbal intelligence is highly developed have an easy time with both written and oral language. They have a natural way with words and an extensive vocabulary, and enjoy rhymes, puns, and telling stories. Skills such as learning a new language, explaining instructions, spelling, and verbal memorization come easily to them.

Logical-Mathematical Intelligence (Number Smart)

Children with highly developed logical-mathematical intelligence are curious about how things work, and enjoy numbers, abstract concepts, and strategy games. They use traditional mathematical reasoning, logic, and scientific thinking, and like to ask questions. They have an easy time understanding numbers and complex calculations and computer programming.

Visual-Spatial Intelligence (Picture Smart)

Children with strong visual intelligence need to be able to see things in order to understand them. Charts, graphs, visual displays and movies are quickly comprehended by them. They enjoy taking apart and reconstructing things and working on puzzles and mazes. Because they have a strong visual memory, a good eye for details and colors, and good eye-hand coordination, many are artistic.

Musical Intelligence (Music Smart)

Children with strong musical intelligence can easily remember melodies and have a high sensitivity to sounds, tones, and music. Their sharp hearing lets them understand a story or lecture without visual aids and tell when music is off-key. They enjoy rhyming, singing, playing an instrument, and composing music. These children tend to sing, hum, or move rhythmically throughout the day.

Kinesthetic Intelligence (Body Smart)

Children with high kinesthetic intelligence learn best by moving and using their body parts. They often excel in sports, acting, and dance. They are highly coordinated and are able to remember things through muscle memory. They enjoy working with their hands, learning things by touch, taking things apart and trying to put them back together, and building things. They often have trouble sitting still and will tap or fidget when required to sit.

Interpersonal Intelligence (People Smart)

Children with strong interpersonal intelligence have lots of friends and enjoy socializing. They are able to create meaningful, lasting relationships with people. They are natural leaders, and are also willing to let others lead. They are sensitive and caring, understand feelings, and help others solve problems. They have strong communication skills and can explain their needs and wants easily.

Intrapersonal Intelligence (Self Smart)

Children with strong intrapersonal intelligence are very independent and self-directed. They have high self-esteem and self-confidence, and are usually introverted, not looking to their peers for approval. They are in tune with their emotions, abilities, goals, and weaknesses. They tend to learn from their own mistakes and successes, and march to the beat of their own drum. They need quiet places for reflection.

Naturalistic Intelligence (Nature Smart)

Children with strong naturalistic intelligence feel connected to nature and prefer being outdoors. They are sensitive toward the environment and other living creatures and enjoy gardening and pets. They are interested in the natural cycles of the world, from animals to astronomy.

Linguistic Intelligence (Word Smart) Learning: Through listening, taking notes, and discussions.
Possible Careers: Teachers, poets, writers, journalists, philosophers, lawyers, and politicians.

Logical-Mathematical Intelligence (Number Smart) Learning: By reasoning, questioning, investigating, and calculating.
Possible Careers: Economists, mathematicians, scientists, programmers, and doctors.

Visual-Spatial Intelligence (Picture Smart) Learning: Through visual displays, charts, pictures, and videos.
Possible Careers: Architects, engineers, mechanics, interior designers, and artists.

Musical Intelligence (Music Smart) Learning: Through rhyming and songs for memorization and working with music playing in the background.
Possible Careers: Musicians, singers, composers, and conductors.

Kinesthetic Intelligence (Body Smart) Learning: Through doing and trying rather than watching or hearing.
Possible Careers: Athletes, performers, dancers, builders, firefighters, and surgeons.

Interpersonal Intelligence (People Smart) Learning: Through discussions and collaborative activities.
Possible Careers: Politicians, teachers, therapists, social workers, and managers.

Intrapersonal Intelligence (Self Smart) Learning: Through independent projects and study, and journal writing.
Possible Careers: Philosophers, researchers, psychologists, writers, and theologians.

Naturalistic Intelligence (Nature Smart) Learning: Through being outdoors in nature or connecting the topic to the natural world.
Possible Careers: Farmers, biologists, conservationists, gardeners, and astronomers.

 TIP: Help your kids understand how they learn best and give them opportunities to develop strengths in as many areas as you can. Love and appreciate their strengths—they are all valuable.

Does my child have to take yearly tests?

"Wisdom is not a product of schooling but of the lifelong attempt to acquire it."
– ALBERT EINSTEIN

Achievement testing has become a hot-button issue in the U.S. Although achievement tests are meant to test the effectiveness of the teachers and the school, it is the children who bear the brunt of testing. Teaching to the test has become more and more the norm in schools, even though research (and common sense) show that it is ineffective and even damaging to the process of learning. Everyone, from the students to the teachers to the administrators, is under a lot of pressure, not to make sure the students are learning to think critically and understand our world, but to do well on a specific test. Some students will do fine in this environment, some teachers work around the constraints to provide excellent teaching, and some schools avoid pressuring their teachers to produce better test scores. Unfortunately, that is not the case for many students, teachers, and schools.

Homeschoolers don't have their paychecks riding on achievement test scores. Some states don't even require an annual test, although many do. This means that we can help our kids learn in the best ways possible, without trying to teach to any particular test. Test scores can become just one source of information on how our kids are doing, rather than the holy grail of achievement.

There are several tests available, and in most states you can choose which one to use to best gauge where your children are educationally. Bear in mind, though, that each test has its downsides. No test is going to accurately show all the skills your children have learned, unless the only thing you've done that year is teach to that particular test. As one of my friends put it, "We did a whole fascinating section on ancient Egyptian mythology this year, but that certainly wasn't covered by any of the tests." Tests are there to give you feedback, and one of the biggest things they give feedback about is how your children take tests. Fortunately, you probably already know what kinds of things they know and where their challenges lie, and a yearly test will most likely confirm that. On the other hand, it may give you useful insight into strengths and challenges that you hadn't seen before.

> **TOM SAYS:** *Testing provides external validation that homeschooling is "working," assuaging fears that the children aren't learning enough. Test scores provide reassurance to unschoolers that children do learn even without curricula, and can be used to bolster confidence in homeschooling when talking with uncertain relatives and friends. There is no need to share actual scores with anyone else, just being able to say that the children are progressing well as shown by external measures is usually enough.*

Our kids have no test anxiety, although that doesn't hold true for every homeschooled kid. I don't have to give them quizzes and tests at all throughout the year if I don't want to—with one exception. In Minnesota we are required to give our students aged seven and up an annual achievement test. There are a variety of approved tests to choose from, and the tests are solely intended for parental feedback. We don't need to report the scores, and generally the tests tell us what we already know about how our students are doing. In some states you do need to report the scores, and if there are significant learning delays then you might need to file an educational plan stating how you are addressing the delays. Some people do use well known tests like the Iowa Basic, but it's not required by our state. We have been happy with the Peabody Individual Achievement Test, which is oral and given by an official tester. Except for the social anxiety our oldest experienced with the very first test, the kids look forward to their testing. In fact, one year they asked if they could have the nice lady over every week so they could test their skills with her! Last year our oldest tried out an online testing service, using the MAP Growth test (Measures of Academic Progress), because the Peabody was getting too easy for him and he enjoyed the challenge. On the other hand, we only chose to do two hour-long sections, math and language, so it was longer and not as comprehensive overall. This year we tried and liked the Woodcock Johnson III test, which is another oral test, and is more challenging in the upper ranges than the Peabody.

The kids actually like oral quizzes like the Brain Quest quiz packs, and we like to sit around and read over them together. I tell them to make their best guesses, that if they're getting more than two-thirds of the questions right then the level is too easy for them and we're not learning anything. This is one major difference in the way we approach learning that helps us avoid test anxiety. One of the things we emphasize in our house is that failing is okay, and making mistakes is actually a good way to learn. There's no penalty for getting something wrong as long as you are trying, and the thing to do is to figure out what went wrong so that you can fix it. I make sure to point out my own mistakes, and we often end up laughing about how silly they can be. Our favorite mistake was when I was reading the Brain Quest science question, "What instrument do you use to look at the stars?" Except I said "stairs" instead of "stars." The kids still laugh about that, and so it's now a family "in" joke. I also remind them of when I made other mistakes, like dropping a full pitcher of lemonade all over the kitchen floor and breaking my favorite pitcher. I usually remind them (and myself) of this when there's been something broken or a big messy accident. Everyone makes mistakes. Just clean up the mess and let it go.

The whole structure of school is set up around making the fewest mistakes possible, and the only way you can feel good about yourself is if you don't make any mistakes. That brings on test anxiety like crazy, and even when the testing is done to assess the teachers and the schools, it's the kids who suffer. If you're already in an environment that stresses perfection, it's almost impossible to avoid being anxious about taking tests unless you're so smart you're not being challenged or you've given up and just don't care. School is all about competition to make the highest grade. Then you can feel superior to other students who didn't score as high as you did and inferior to those who did better than you.

I made very good grades in school, and that evoked a lot of envy from other students. I had enough kids say, "I hate you!" when they found out that I got an A on a test that I learned to pretend not to be so smart, and just say I did okay on a test, or emphasize the only thing I got wrong. Once when I got the highest score in the class, a 98 out of 100, the teacher asked me what my score was in front of everyone. Then he told everyone in the class to add two points to their scores. I cringed, knowing that it would make plenty of them like me less. I didn't have anxiety about taking the tests, just about other people finding out my grades.

Unfortunately, even kids who have always been homeschooled may have test anxiety, and those who are coming to homeschooling after going to conventional school may have an especially hard time with tests. Even oral tests like the Peabody can be very stressful for people with dyslexia, since they do include focusing and reading components. Kids who are overwhelmed or simply fatigued may give up rather than asking for a break or for more time to think about a question. Fortunately there is much more leeway in homeschool testing in the ability to choose which test works best, to take extra time when it's needed, and to support the kids in advocating for themselves when they are at their limits. Mindfulness practices can help both parents and kids not only to be aware of when those limits are being reached but also to be calmer about the whole testing process. Our test administrator recommends the workbook *Mindfulness Skills for Kids and Teens* by Debra Burdick.

Test-taking is a skill that can be learned, but as with any learning, it doesn't need to take a long time. There is no need to subject your children to tedious bubble-filling tests year after year just because they will need to know how to take them at some point. Of course, if the kids actually enjoy doing them, go for it. There are strategies for answering multiple choice and true/false questions that can be learned fairly quickly. Learning how a particular test is scored also makes a difference—sometimes it's better to leave something blank if you don't know the answer, and sometimes it's better to guess. It's good to know how to take tests, and it's also good to know what kind of tests you do best on. But standardized testing has very little relevance to real life and to determining which people succeed. Indeed, grades in high school and college don't necessarily show who will be successful and who will not. So take these tests with a grain of salt. Yes, the kids should try to do well on them, but use them as one method of assessment among many rather than taking them as an indicator of success or failure.

TIP: Testing says more about taking tests than about intelligence; daily observation and involvement is the best way to know where your kids stand. Consider your kids' learning styles when choosing a test, and spend a little time preparing them for it. Test-taking is a skill like any other, and can be learned in a fairly short period of time.

What about extracurriculars?

"We can get too easily bogged down in the academic part of homeschooling, a relatively minor part of the whole, which is to raise competent, caring, literate, happy people."
– DIANE FLYNN KEITH, AUTHOR OF *CARSCHOOLING*

How do you choose which activities to add into your day? It's all dependent on your family's interests and your child's capabilities.

First of all, don't over-schedule! Some of the best learning comes during free time and open-ended play. In the Twin Cities, there are so many homeschool-specific activities, all of them temptingly fun and educational, that we could be out participating in multiple activities every weekday. I have found that for our family, less is more, and choosing our activities with care and mindfulness is important. We have a few regular groups that the boys enjoy, and every couple of months we add in something special like a play or tour. Anything more becomes too exhausting, both mentally and physically, since it's on top of classwork and music and therapy.

Next, try a wide variety of things over time, and let your kids lead the way. If something interests them, focus on it for however long it holds their interest. There are various schools of thought when it comes to making kids finish what they start. I generally ask them to give it a good try, but if they really don't like a project or class they don't have to finish it. Forcing someone to do something they aren't enjoying is a good way to make them dislike it more. On the other hand, people grow to like things they are good at. It's a balancing act between encouraging them to continue building new skills and allow-ing them to quit doing something they dislike. I think the key is to determine whether they're just not good at something yet or if they actively dislike it for some other reason. If the other kids are mean, or the coach is discouraging, or the piano teacher just isn't explaining things well, feel free to leave and find people who will help your kids build up their skills and confidence instead. You may have to dig a little to find out what the real problem is, or watch the interactions in a group closely, because kids aren't always able to articulate why they dislike something.

One of the things I love best about homeschooling is the amount of time we have for a well-rounded education, including learning to pursue one's own interests without the need for prodding by adults. Last year we added in piano lessons for our two oldest. I told the boys that I wanted them to take a year of music so they have a grounding in it. If they wanted to continue after that, fine, but I wasn't attached to it. I just wanted them to practice ten minutes a day, which I wrote on our daily whiteboard list, and give it their best shot. About four weeks after we started, my oldest changed his time on the whiteboard to 30 minutes daily, and a week or so later to 60 minutes. Turns out he loves learning music, and going to the music store to buy new sheet music totally makes his day. He finished six of the seven course levels within the first year. (His goal was to finish all seven.) His teacher said she'd never had any student in 20 years accomplish that. Not so much with his younger brother, who practices enough to satisfy himself while leaving plenty of time to pursue his various other interests. I let him stop taking lessons a couple of months early because he really wasn't enjoying the lessons, but he doesn't plan to give up piano. In fact, he and his brother brainstormed together to make a plan that doesn't include lessons. He will choose pieces to learn that he likes, as opposed to just going through every piece in the books. Then he will ask his brother to help him master parts that he needs help with. I thought that was a great idea! He avoids the part he doesn't like (being told what to do), and pursues his musical education on his own terms. I suspect he will learn a lot more that way than if I made him take lessons he hates. And if he ever decides he wants more advanced coaching we can do lessons again.

Our kids get a lot of extracurricular activities from our co-op. We originally joined because of an excellent math teacher for our oldest, but since then have added in a number of fun things as well. We just have to be conscious of the budget, and make sure that they really are engaged in their classes. There are all kinds of opportunities, from foreign language to fencing to art to knitting, as well as more academic classes such as biology, chemistry, writing, and history.

Generally I make some suggestions and then let them choose, but last year I insisted that our oldest take a ballroom dance class, for a number of reasons. First and foremost, it's a social skills class for him, and it gets him out of his introverted mindset. Second, it teaches physical grace and coordination. And finally, I think everyone should know at least the basics of ballroom dancing. It helped that a good friend of his started taking the classes the year before and enjoyed them, so our son was much less resistant to it after a year of hearing how much fun his friend was having. I was pleasantly surprised to have him ask to go to Sunday nights at a ballroom dance venue with a live band, and it is lovely to watch him dancing with young ladies out on the floor. Most of the people there are middle aged and up, except for a fairly large contingent of young homeschoolers from the co-op. He signed up for ballroom dance classes again this year without any prompting from me.

While a lot of people consider extracurricular activities to be classes, and we certainly have done plenty of classes, your choices are much wider than that. Look around to find groups that meet to support each other doing things as diverse as Lego robotics, rock climbing, German discussion, orienteering, photography, and raising chickens. Local 4-H clubs and Scouts teach lots of practical and leadership skills, book clubs abound, and the YMCA has swim teams complete with competitions. Your family also might like to do projects or hobbies together or individually, instead of with a group. We know a couple of families who go geocaching on a regular basis as part of their extracurricular program. Others pursue individual excellence in areas that range from baking to origami. My geologist dad took our group on a field trip to hunt for fossils. Ask around to find people who can help foster your kids' extracurricular interests.

All three of our boys have had an interest in doing stage magic, and we have facilitated this with stacks of books and some DVDs from the library, plus a couple of magic kits. We have watched free magic shows at the library, and have found some on Netflix. This fall we took the boys to see the illusionist Adam Trent so they could see someone on the big stage. Although magic is not the usual extra-curricular, it builds coordination and fine motor skills, and helps build confidence in presenting to a group. Our oldest kept a group of preschool and elementary aged children oohing and aahing for ten minutes at a birthday party last summer with his magic tricks.

Fit your family's extracurricular activities to your own circum-stances. Your budget and your kids' individual interests should dictate what your family pursues, not ideas about what extracurriculars "ought to" look like. Also, if budgetary reasons are holding you back, remember to look for scholarships. Some places offer academic or need-based scholarships for extracurricular activities.

TIP: Try out a variety of things to find the extracurriculars that motivate your kids and fit with your family budget. Look for local or online groups for support, or start one yourself.

How will my child learn to drive?

"Always focus on the front windshield and not the review mirror."
– COLIN POWELL

No need to worry, most places have accommodations for wannabe drivers who are not in high school. Some states allow parents to be the primary driving teachers, and some require formal classes. Sometimes it will be community education classes, sometimes it will be night school, and sometimes the school system will let homeschoolers take driver's ed through a high school. If all else fails, there are private driving schools, although they tend to be more expensive. The American Automobile Association, AAA, offers driving classes in some areas.

Check with local homeschool groups to see what they recommend, or if you are the first in the group to hit this milestone, try calling the school district for more information. They may have suggestions or a list of approved classes. If you live in a very small town, you might need to commute to a larger community for driver ed if the laws or your own comfort level prohibit parent-taught education. This website lists requirements for each state under their tab High School Info, then Curriculum: LetsHomeschoolHighSchool.com

Please don't just leave the training to the professionals, though. A number of different studies have shown that parental involvement is the most important factor in teaching teens safe driving practices. Check out the National Driver Training Institute's parent-taught driving program at usdrivertraining.com, run by Wayne Tully, who has worked to change driver training laws in 28 states. Driver education articles on hslda.com discuss a study done by UC-Colorado Springs in 2000 where students who went through this program with their parents were compared with teen drivers who hadn't done the program. These students were shown to have 80% fewer tickets for speeding, 75% fewer tickets for driving under the influence, 60% fewer accidents, 50% fewer injuries from accidents, and no fatalities compared to 1 in every 100 teens who hadn't taken the program. Unfortunately, this study is often quoted but never referenced; I haven't been able to track down the original research. Nevertheless it seems important to pass along, as it matches up with what other studies and common sense tell us: parents need to be involved with driver education, even if they aren't the primary teachers.

Teens also need many more hours of practice behind the wheel than classes are able to provide. They need us in the car with them to help them develop safe driving habits. And as parents who learned to drive some time ago, we can pass on outdated or even wrong information if we're not up to date ourselves. A friend of mine just recently took her son in for his driving test, and apparently that state's booklet on driving rules was outdated. She had to find an actual driving school for him so that he could pass the test and get his license, because he failed to observe some traffic laws that neither of them knew about.

TIP: Make sure you are following the legal requirements of your city, county and state. There are plenty of places that offer driver education, or you may be able to teach it yourself.

What if my child has special needs?

"Special needs homeschooling is the same as any other homeschooling. It may be more time consuming, but you're still right there responding to their educational and emotional needs."
– ERIN MCKINNEY SOUSTER, HOMESCHOOL PARENT AND ORGANIZER

Many families with special needs children who feel that those needs aren't being met within the school system are choosing to homeschool. As one woman in an online support group put it, "I can't possibly do a worse job than they did last year." That helped bolster her confidence that she and her family could homeschool successfully. All children benefit from individual attention and from education tailored specifically to them, children with special needs doubly so. It is very easy to get labeled in the school system, positively or negatively, and very hard for impressionable children to understand that a label doesn't define them.

Even when teachers are trying their best there aren't always the resources to provide what each student needs. A good friend of ours has a gifted and severely dyslexic son who was promised special help for his pre-algebra class through his Individual Educational Plan (IEP). Unfortunately, the school was highly understaffed that year and there was no one available to give him the support he needed. He failed the class, and spent the summer being privately tutored instead. Homeschooling can provide that kind of individual attention regularly, as opposed to remedially.

Special needs encompasses a wide range of differing needs. It covers everything from developmental delays to gifted and talented people, and every individual has delays and gifts to one degree or another. Even if I were an expert in one of those areas, I'm not an expert on your child. But you are. This section is here to convey some broad ideas about how people approach homeschooling with a variety of special needs kids, to let you know that plenty of people are doing it and so can you.

There are many different approaches to homeschooling someone with special needs, and if something isn't working, feel free to change it however you can. What works for your family will depend on the types of support your child needs, the needs and the support of the rest of the family, your insurance, the supportiveness of the local school system, and especially the mental and emotional resilience of you as parents. Finding a good homeschooling support group for special needs families will make a huge difference. By and large the homeschoolers we hang out with have been very tolerant of the different needs of other families, and haven't experienced any problems with bullying or even rudeness. Unfortunately, that's not always the case, so check out a variety of groups to find one that fits your family's situation. And bear in mind that adolescents may feel the need to push boundaries by being rude and insulting; otherwise nice kids can sometimes slip over the edge into meanness when in groups. If there's an issue, don't let it fester. Let people know when something goes over the edge. Respectfully, please, but don't tolerate behavior that negatively impacts your child. Help the other kids (and their families) understand the effects they are having, and ask them to be respectful. Also help your kids to advocate for themselves, not tolerating mean behavior. Most people will act accordingly when they realize they will be held accountable for their actions. If not, go elsewhere.

Some people get their kids tested so they can get IEPs for those kids, which can help in getting extra services in some states. Yes, even for homeschoolers. Other states won't do much at all to provide help for homeschoolers through the school system. It's an individual choice for parents. If it will help you get access to resources you need, go for it—jump through the hoops and do all the testing. If it isn't going to make a difference in access, but it will help you design an educational program by knowing exactly what's going on, again, go for it. If you know what's going on with your kids and how you best want to help them, do whatever you feel is best for your family. I will say that occupational therapy tests found a number of deficits in all three of our boys that I was not expecting. For one thing, they all have balance issues that I never would have picked up on since they aren't clumsy and generally like to climb trees and are all over playground equipment. Now we can get them help we didn't even know they needed.

There is a whole spectrum of ways to homeschool special needs kids, just as there is a whole spectrum of special needs. In truth, there are no "average" kids. Nobody is going to be developmentally average in every area; everyone will be ahead or behind their cohorts' averages to some degree. Special needs kids just tend to be more ahead of or behind the curve than most, and they need more attention and help from the adults in their lives. In plenty of cases kids will have both delays and excesses, for example being extremely bright and having dyslexia. Homeschooling will let you tailor your education to your child, giving extra help and therapies where needed and letting them progress at their own rate in every area.

One family we know homeschools because their child has congenital heart and lung problems, and sending her to school was medically impossible when she was younger. They also didn't want to expose her to the germs her siblings would bring home from school, and so the whole family learned at home in order to keep their sister's hospital stays to a minimum. They still went on as many outings as they could, and are continuing to enjoy homeschooling now that she is healthier. I won't say it's less likely that they would pick up germs at a homeschool outing than in school. However, a point worth making is that school systems are set up to encourage parents to send kids to school as many days as possible, rather than keeping them home as long as necessary. Homeschoolers have the option of staying home until everyone is well.

I know of more than one homeschooling family that adopted a special needs child; one of them told me that her son, now well-adjusted, was originally so behaviorally challenged that the family mostly stayed home for a couple of years after he was adopted. They made sure they had a safe and loving environment for him, only visiting with a friend or two at a time and avoiding group situations that overwhelmed him. He also got the therapeutic services he needed, and by the time we met them he had become a cheerful, confident, and outgoing young man. Sometimes you may need your kids to be hermits for a little while; just make sure that you don't turn into a hermit yourself, and that it's only temporary.

Another family has an adopted child who is sweet and enthusiastic and artistic, and cannot process math functions well. In that regard, their main goal is for him to be able to balance a checkbook as an adult, but that doesn't define his education. He is exposed to all kinds of science and art and literature that he might not get on a remedial track in a school setting.

There are also plenty of families with kids on the autism spectrum who homeschool. After going to public school for several years, one boy with Asperger's made his first ever friends in our group. It was great for his confidence and his happiness, and he brought some wonderful enthusiasm to the group. I remember how touched his parents were during the first birthday party he had after quitting school. The entire homeschool group came—real friends who were happy to be celebrating his birthday with him. He had never had that experience before, and he was overjoyed. Because many homeschoolers already feel like non-conformists, peer pressure to conform tends to be much lower and along with that comes acceptance of a wider range of behaviors and personality types. Of course, that depends on the group; secular homeschoolers have generally been more open and accepting, in our experience.

One family we know with two children didn't intend to homeschool at all, but they found their gifted child wasn't well served by the school system. The teachers in the regular classes had to focus on those children with educational or behavioral problems, and couldn't give the student the attention he needed. Their approach was to give him extra homework to keep him occupied, but it was more of the same stuff he had already breezed through. The mom said that the gifted program in that school was filled with entitled, snobbish, rude kids, ones who were disrespectful even to the teachers and their own parents. They decided to try homeschooling instead, which is working really well for their son, not only because they can give him plenty of mental stimulation but also because he gets to have plenty of like-minded friends. He goes to a social co-op for gifted homeschoolers, with fun classes and time for socializing, so that he doesn't feel singled out for being the smart one. Their other child attends a language immersion school, which fits his needs nicely.

A Little Bit About Homeschooling with Special Needs

Aza Âû Donnelly, MHA Special Needs Coordinator

When my kids were diagnosed with autism, and a host of other things, I finally laid down the dream of gentle homeschooling that would produce prodigies. We hunkered down and figured out what they actually needed and actually wanted. How do we help keep them safe, facilitate independence, and continue to foster a love of learning that they can take with them for a lifetime? We chose to continue with unschooling, others choose a different path. Part of why unschooling works for us is because both of my kids can be resistant to requests, changes, leaving the house, certain fine and gross motor tasks. My dyslexic daughter refused to be taught how to read, she is teaching herself, slowly but surely. Had I forced her, I don't think she would be reading yet. My other child hated all fine motor skills, including writing, but has a deep desire to draw and animate. A happy consequence of that is that he now has beautiful writing.

My husband reminds me a lot that we need to be process-oriented rather than goal-oriented. I consider myself a facilitator. I provide the materials and how-to guides, and let them do the rest. Because my kids are resistant, I don't force anything. There are practical health and safety things, of course, but if I try to force things, they shut down and/or melt down.

On all days, we let the kids set the pace as much as is responsibly possible (certain things must get done.) If it's a great day, we will choose together what we want to spend our time and energy doing. Same if it's a rough day. We just do what we can to keep ourselves afloat. Sometimes the kids make choices that make me nervous; a kid having a hard day that decides they want to go out shopping... As parents we know how that can end, but I have learned how to prepare myself and turn that into a self-discovery moment. Sometimes shopping was exactly what that kid needed, and sometimes as soon as we get in the car they realize it was a poor choice for them.

Being able to be self-determine has many, many, positives. But the one that is the most important to me is safety. Self-determined kids know their limits, they are less likely to put themselves in situations where they feel unsafe, they are less likely to be bullied and abused, they are more likely to make choices that work for them in any given situation. Self-determined kids know their strengths and weaknesses (sometimes that changes from day to day) and it paves the way for real self-advocacy, and advocacy for others.

Every child and every family is going to have their own special circumstances and needs. My child can make responsible decisions around how to spend their allowance, but needs help with healthy food choices. But the more decisions we can let them make, they better off they will be in the long run.

As you can see, a wide variety of families are successfully homeschooling their special needs children. If you would really like to homeschool, please don't let the extra attention that special needs children require stop you. Approach special needs homeschooling with intentionality and mindfulness, and bring your child into the discussion of what would be best for him or her. And remember that you don't have to be the sole provider of attention and support for your child. Look for programs, groups, and friends who suit the circumstances of your family and yourself, and who can help you throughout your journey.

TIP: You are the expert on your child and can respond quickly when something needs to be changed. Get the support your kids need to help them learn and grow, and get support for yourself from others handling the same challenges.

Resources and References

A2ZHomeschooling.com - A huge compilation of homeschooling resources

affordabletests.com - MAP Growth online test

aspergerexperts.com - Advice from young adults with Asperger's on managing daily life

caph.gmu.edu - George Mason University center for public health study on driver training: "Young Drivers: A Study of Policies and Practices."

clickschooling.com - Sign up for a daily email with a link to a free educational resource

educents.com - Discounts on educational toys, movies, books, etc.

HomeschoolAdventures.org - Minnesota resources for groups and classes and outings

homeschoolbuyersco-op.org - Discounts on educational programs and gear, plus student IDs

letshomeschoolhighschool.com - Resources for high school age homeschoolers

nessy.com - Resources for dyslexic students

PaperbackSwap.com - Swap your books for others for the price of shipping

PearceOnEarth.com - Travel homeschool blog plus free resource guide

kids.nwf.org - Ranger Rick magazines and games for kids ages 0-12

kiwico.com - Activity boxes for kids 3 and up

shop.Cricketmedia.com - Magazines for kids 6 months and up - history, literature, science, etc.

usdrivertraining.com - Drivers ed program

www.WeiserEducational.com - Easy to read material on more advanced topics youtube.com - TedEd, Crash Course, Minute Earth, Minute Physics, VSauce, Brain Scoop, Physics Girl, Veritasium, Science Max, etc.

zoobooks.com - In-depth magazines about animals for kids 0-12

Brain Quest workbooks and quiz decks, grades Pre-K through 6th, Workman Publishing

Carschooling: Over 350 Entertaining Games & Activities to Turn Travel Time into Learning Time - For Kids Ages 4 to 17, Diane Flynn Keith, Homefires Press, 2nd Edition (August 23, 2009)

Growing Up Mindful: Essential Practices to Help Children, Teens, and Families Find Balance, Calm, and Resilience, Christopher Willard, Sounds True, 1st Edition (June 1, 2016

Homeschool Your Child for Free: More than 1,400 Smart, Effective, and Practical Resources for Educating Your Family at Home, Laura Maery Gold & Joan M. Zielinsky, Three Rivers Press, 2nd Updated, Revised Edition (August 4, 2009)

Mindfulness Skills for Kids and Teens: A Workbook for Clinicians and Clients with 154 Tools, Techniques, Activities and Worksheets, Debra Burdick, PESI Publishing & Media, Workbook Edition (September 1, 2014)

Multiple Intelligences: The Theory In Practice, Howard E. Gardner, Basic Books, 1st Edition (April 20, 1993)

Raising Your Spirited Child: A Guide for Parents Whose Child Is More Intense, Sensitive, Perceptive, Persistent, and Energetic, Mary Sheedy Kurcinka, William Morrow Paperbacks, 3rd Edition (September 8, 2015)

Sitting Still Like a Frog: Mindfulness Exercises for Kids (and Their Parents), Eline Snel, Shambhala, Paperback/CD Edition (December 3, 2013)

The Unschooled Mind: How Children Think and How Schools Should Teach, Howard E. Gardner, Basic Books, 2nd Edition (March 29, 2011)

Sexual Education

"Nothing in life is to be feared, it is only to be understood. Now is the time to understand more, so that we may fear less."

– MARIE CURIE

This section became so long, and included so many resources, that it became a chapter of its own. It's an important subject that a lot of people are uncomfortable talking about, and it deserves attention.

The best way to go about sex education is to start when your kids are young. Discussing sex ed is also a great time to practice mindfulness. Pay attention to what their actual questions are, rather than what you think they are. Notice where you start to get uncomfortable, and see if you can get beyond the discomfort so your kids will feel okay asking you these questions. Answer their questions about where babies come from as matter-of-factly as you can, and read them factual books that are age appropriate. Do make sure to leave them on the bookshelf where they are easily accessible. I remember my dad telling me he had some books that I could read for more information when I was 13. I really wanted to read them, but I never figured out where he had them squirreled away. And I was too embarrassed to ask. I have listed a lot of books at the end of this section, along with the publisher's age recommendations. Please look through them yourself first to make sure your child's maturity level is on par with the recommendations, and also be prepared for your child to spring a question or two on you. If you aren't sure about how something works, don't wing it. Look it up yourself first, or find out about it together. There are also useful videos for more visual learners but generally those that aren't completely boring are for preteens and up. There is a striking dearth of good sex ed videos for younger children.

Take this as a great opportunity to help your kids learn what's really going on with their bodies and with those of the opposite sex. Factually complete sex education is much more effective than abstinence-only education, not only at raising the age of first sexual experience, but also in being very effective in preventing teen pregnancies and the transmission of sexually transmitted diseases.

Many people unfamiliar with the research fear that thorough sex education will encourage kids to have more sex. A good synopsis of the research can be found at AdvocatesForYouth.org, under their Publications section. From their Comprehensive Sex Education: Research and Results: "Research clearly shows that comprehensive sex education programs do not encourage teens to start having sexual intercourse; do not increase the frequency with which teens have intercourse; and do not increase the number of a teen's sexual partners. At the same time, evaluations of publicly funded abstinence-only programs have repeatedly shown no positive changes in sexual behaviors over time. Young people need honest, effective sex education—not ineffective, shame-based abstinence-only programs."

I am baffled by the sheer misinformation and wrong ideas that are still common among people, from those old myths that you can't get pregnant if it's your first time to young women tweeting about boyfriends who want to know why they can't just "hold" their periods like urine. Why do these kinds of misapprehensions about basic body functions continue to persist in this day and age? Most likely because it's uncomfortable for most of us to discuss it; the biology of it all has been so entwined with titillation, guilt, and shame that it's hard for us to get past it. We need to make the effort, but it can definitely be an effort.

To me, telling teens to wait until marriage without explaining how things work and how to keep themselves safe is like telling children that roads are unsafe and that they will be able to go on roads when they get their drivers' licenses. Imagine if you never explained to your children why it's not safe to stand in the street, if you never helped them learn to look and listen for cars, if you only let them ride a bike on the sidewalk around the block. That road will become forbidden fruit, scary and tempting, and they will have no knowledge of how to keep themselves safe if they ever need to cross one or even ride their bikes down to the store. And how tricky would it be to learn to drive, knowing nothing about driving patterns and stop signs? Teaching kids the rules of the road and ways to keep safe navigating around the neighborhood will not make them run out and steal a car to drive around, and teaching them how bodies work and ways to keep safe and healthy will not make them run out and have sex. It will likely also help them have fulfilling relationships later with their long-term partners if they know what to expect and how to help each other have a mutually satisfying time.

A recent study done in the UK found something that seems contrary to this claim: As schools cut funding for sex education, pregnancy rates dropped. To me, this doesn't say that sex ed doesn't work at all. It says that learning sex ed *in school* doesn't work for everyone, at least in the UK. Also bear in mind that it *wasn't* replaced by abstinence-only education. If I found out that the kids' school dropped sex ed, I would be highly motivated to teach them everything they needed to know at home. Guess what? Learning the facts of life from someone with a vested interest in their kids' sexual health might be more effective than getting it while sitting in classroom.

Kids want and need to know the truth of how things work in their world, including the human body. If teens have the knowledge to make an informed decision, rather than hoping things turn out well or not even knowing the consequences of their actions, then it is easier to choose a safe path. Please don't assume that if you don't discuss it with them then they won't know anything about it! They will find out any way they can, and there is a lot of misinformation and even information that can be dangerous to their health out there. The CDC website has several pages devoted to sexual health for adolescents. If you really don't feel comfortable, or knowledgeable, enough to help your kids with sex ed, look into the Unitarian church's program, Our Whole Life (OWL), which has a lovely comprehensive curriculum for various ages. Feel free to mention that sex feels good, and doesn't have to lead to pregnancy or disease, rather than just focusing on the potentially negative aspects; you'll set them on the road to healthy relationships when the time comes. Knowing their own bodies and what is pleasurable will also help them, now and down the road, and sex with oneself is the safest sex there is.

One thing parents worry about is keeping kids safe from molestation. This often doesn't fall under the category of sex education, but

I think it should. It starts with your being respectful of them (and yourself) when they are young. Don't force them to hug or kiss people if it makes them uncomfortable; offer a wave, a handshake, or a high five as an alternative. Let them know that they can always talk to you, and that it is okay to say no to things they are uncomfortable with. And remember, strangers are very rarely the problem. Scaring children away from strangers can be counterproductive, because some day they may need to approach a stranger to get directions, order an ice cream at a store, or even get help because somebody is trying to hurt them. Instead, coach them on what is and isn't appropriate to share with strangers, like personal information, contact information, and if their parents are home when answering the phone. They can look for help from moms with kids or a manager in a store if they are ever lost or in a bad situation.

One good way to help kids exercise caution is to talk about the behavior of "tricky" people. Tricky people might single a kid out for special treats, or act like a best friend when it's not age-appropriate, ask for help in finding a lost cat or dog, ask a kid to keep secrets, sympathize with a kid against their parents, or offer to do something really fun that would separate them from the group or from you. You can point things out in books or videos as well as just discussing them. The witch in C.S. Lewis's *The Lion, the Witch and the Wardrobe* exhibits a number of these characteristics - she treats Edmund as someone special, gives him treats, asks for personal information, offers him more treats if he does something for her, and tells him to keep it all a secret, separating him from any support from his family. A police officer who spoke at our parenting class suggested that we use the word "surprise" instead of "secret" when planning things like birthday parties. A surprise is something that is fun and that will be revealed soon, just not immediately. Don't have secrets in your family.

Another important thing here is to give all body parts their correct names. Not only will it help your kids know their functions (and know that it's okay to discuss body parts rather than having parts that should not be spoken about except in euphemisms), but also it will help them correctly communicate important things about their own bodies.

Finally, if your child suddenly starts using euphemisms like "cupcake" or "snake" to describe their genitalia, it will send an immediate warning signal that should be pursued. I recommend watching The Safe Side videos on strangers and on internet safety with your kids. They're corny and fun and filled with good information, although they are far from comprehensive. Safely Ever After is a great website for more information, as is the book *Protecting the Gift* by Gavin de Becker. I was surprised to find out how many online games have a chat component to them; that function allows people access to your child even at home, and can be fertile ground for grooming kids for exploitation. Make sure you have regular discussions with your kids as to warning signs that the other person is being inappropriate, and that they know they can ask you about anything that feels uncomfortable to them.

The Super Ten, Play-It-Safe Rules For Kids and Grownups!

SafelyEverAfter.com

1. I am the boss of my body!

2. I know my name, address, and phone number, and my parents' cell phone numbers, too.

3. Safe grownups don't ask kids for help! (They should ask other grownups for assistance.)

4. I never go anywhere with or take anything from someone I don't know, no matter what they say.

5. I always check first and get permission before: I go anywhere, get into a car, change my plans, or accept some kind of treat, even if it's with someone I know. If I can't check first, then the answer is NO!

6. Everybody's bathing suit areas are private. No private parts "touching games" allowed; I can say STOP even to a grownup or bigger kid.

7. I don't have to be polite if someone makes me feel scared or uncom-

fortable. It's okay to say NO… even to a grownup, if I have to.

8. I don't keep secrets… especially if they make me feel scared or uneasy. (Nobody should tell a child to keep a secret from their parents, especially a secret about their bodies.)

9. If I ever get lost in a public place, I can freeze and yell, or go to a Mom with kids and ask for help.

10. I will always pay attention to my special Inner Voice, especially if I get an "uh-oh" feeling.

Also, don't avoid discussing homosexuality, as it will help kids recognize something as sexual that they might not otherwise. Be very careful here to differentiate between molestation and consensual adult relations. Consider the science behind homosexuality before discussing it as a "lifestyle choice." It's not a choice. If you yourself can't change who you are attracted to, neither can anyone else. Our culture is so biased against homosexuality and transgender issues that nobody who actually had a choice would choose it on a whim.

Bear in mind that one or more of your kids' friends will be homosexual, if statistics have anything to say about it. (Numbers range from 2% to 10% of every population, across cultures, depending on the study.) Condemning or demonizing homosexuality and transgenderism won't make it go away, but it can drive people away. Your kids' friends may or may not be in a situation where they can be open about it, which can be even more challenging. Be someone your kids can talk to about their friends, even if it's an uncomfortable conversation for you. Your kid might even be that one in ten to fifty, with all that comes along with it (on top of the hormone-riddled confusion of adolescence). Make sure they know that you will always love them and that they can talk to you without being judged negatively. Otherwise they will go elsewhere for information and support, and not only will you be cut out of that part of their lives, they may be getting misinformation that could be harmful. Remember that any derogatory terms that you apply to others will be taken to heart by your own kids, either to perpetuate that disdain of others or to become self-loathing if applied to themselves.

Why Do They Act That Way?
David Walsh, pp 109-110

"Brain science can help adolescents and parents sort through the confusion around sexual orientation, help eliminate any shame, and confront discrimination. Same-sex orientation is not new. Anthropologists have shown that homosexuality has been part of human cultures throughout recorded history. In fact same-sex attraction is not even unique to humans. Scientists have observed it in as many as sixty different animal species. Sexual orientation, heterosexual or homosexual, has its origins in the brain, and they are very complex... Like heterosexuals, gays and lesbians discover how their brain is wired for sexual attraction as they mature. They are not recruited, seduced, or taught to be homosexual."

As your kids get older, try to keep the lines of communication open about sex, even when it seems like they don't want to talk about it with you. One suggestion that makes sense is to err on the side of extra information. In other words, give kids slightly more information than they ask for about sex, and let them tell you what's enough. It's better than giving them insufficient information, which runs the risk of and leaving them feeling uninformed. Just don't go overboard and overwhelm them with anything they're not ready for. Another thing that works well in our family is to talk with them while driving. It can be a lot easier to chat about embarrassing things when you're sitting side by side (or front and back) without the need to make eye contact than it is having a heart-to-heart, face-to-face conversation at the table.

Media outlets generally portray relationships and sex unrealistically; the best defense is to get your kids to think critically about pop culture. Keep commenting on things you see in movies and ads, and ask questions to make sure they're thinking for themselves rather than just taking everything at face value. I tend to refer to scantily clad cartoon girls in video game ads as "anti-gravity girls" because they are so unrealistic and their breasts defy gravity. That helps the boys to differentiate titillating ads from reality, or so I hope.

I've never really liked romantic comedies, but it wasn't until I read an article recently that I realized why they always make me uncomfortable. They are all based on the premise of miscommunication and even straight up lying, on people pretending they're someone they're not until the other person decides they like them before finally revealing who they really are at the end. That's a stupid way to start a relationship; counter that with examples of how real people have actually formed strong relationships.

Another thing worth mentioning is how media portrays reluctant dates turning into relationships after one person shows how desired the other is, pursues the other person doggedly enough, or makes a grand enough gesture. This is not a recipe for a strong relationship, it's a recipe for date rape, stalking, or just embarrassing yourself in front of a lot of people. Relationships should be between people who are both interested, who respect each other, and who are willing to communicate openly and honestly. It's okay to give someone who doesn't know you very well a chance to know you better; just keep checking in to make sure you're not becoming pushy. And grand gestures can be great if you already know the other person likes or loves you. Just don't expect such gestures to sway someone who's not that into you.

A lot of attention has been paid to the slogan, "No means no." That's worth mentioning, but it doesn't go far enough. Turn it on its head: "Yes means yes." That is, give and get specific, explicit agreement on everything. Not only will this avoid inadvertent date rape, it may well lead to more discussion, a deeper relationship, more satisfaction for all parties involved, and possibly a friendship rather than a sexual relationship. It goes both ways. Most cultures presume that guys always want to have sex, and so there is a lot of pressure on them to live up to that, whether they are ready for it or not. Make sure everybody is fully on board before proceeding.

Media also tends to portray instant relationships, where people hit it off with sparks right from the start, fall into bed together, and immediately have fulfilling sex. Let kids know that being friends is a good thing, that instant attraction may or may not lead to friendship and long-term relationships, and that good sex takes practice. In fact, not all good relationships start with fireworks. When my husband and I first met, I liked him but wasn't swept away. He's much more reserved than I am, and at the beginning there were more awkward moments than sharing of confidences. As we spent more time together and got to know each other, he really grew on me. He's quietly steadfast, smart, funny, patient, and willing to work through problems. Instead of fireworks, I got a nice warm fire.

Social media is another way that kids are exposed to inappropriate information and misinformation about sex, and they can easily be pushed beyond their comfort zone. When kids are old enough to start using a smart phone, texting, and participating in social media, have some serious talks with them about it. A great source of advice and pointers is *iRules* by Janell Hofmann. It discusses the detailed and instructive rules that the author wrote in the form of an agreement between her and her son when he got his first smart phone.

Check in with your kids about internet use, talk to them about why you would like to know their passwords, and suggest that nobody use the internet in their rooms. I haven't been able to talk my husband into putting down his phone, which he has on at bedtime and first thing in the morning, but the boys know I leave my phone downstairs, and I've talked to them about why I want the bedroom to be about sleeping. It's a lot easier to get decent sleep if your brain associates your bedroom and especially being in bed with sleeping and not with the dopamine hits we all get when winning game levels and collecting Facebook likes. We installed a nighttime color filter (f.lux) on the screens and shut them down an hour before bedtime so that it doesn't interfere with the boys' sleep patterns, or mine. We have our wifi on a timer, so that the internet is shut down at night. That's right, not even the parents can check Facebook or watch the news after 9:00 p.m.

When you think your teen is ready for it, and he or she is probably ready earlier than you think, consider introducing them to the scarleteen.com website. It includes straight talk for contemporary teens about sex and sexuality, and it pulls no punches. Or if you prefer, buy them a book like *S.E.X.* by Heather Corinna. It's comprehensive and filled with things people need to know as they become adults. You may not agree with everything it has to say, and in that case use it as a discussion topic rather than banning the information. The information (and misinformation) is out there, easy to find and often discussed among their peers. It's better to have factual information readily available than to go searching for it on the fly and risk accessing sketchy websites that may lead to hardcore pornography and malware. Unfortunately, almost all the pornography out there on the internet these days is hardcore, violent, non-consensual porn. Friends of ours have a tween who was looking up something for a school report. When he typed in the website name wrong, he got a site that downloaded a porn photo onto his computer and locked it so that he couldn't get the photo to go away. They had to take the laptop to a computer repair shop and have a chat with the police. The thing about such traumatizing images as that photo is that you can never un-see them.

Finally, remember that sex and sexuality should be a joyful part of a person's life and not anything that is associated with shame, guilt, or pain. Try to impart that tenor when talking to your kids. Sure, there are things to be careful about, and decisions to be made that can affect their lives pretty seriously. But our bodies are beautiful gifts, and they should be respected and enjoyed.

TIP: Be open and honest, use factual terms, leave age-appropriate resources within reach, and check in on internet use regularly. Keep the lines of communication open, your kids will grow up before you're ready for it.

References and Resources for Sexual Education

YouTube videos for kids about child abuse:

https://www.youtube.com/channel/UCdC2_Ejij_BxbNkHhzatEAw

YouTube channels for sex education:

WellCast's Selfies playlist for early to later adolescents
https://www.youtube.com/
playlist?list=PLqldimk4xUgIIwDECvjhuBn01UbtFTKC5

Crash Course's Anatomy and Physiology class - the Reproductive System in 4 parts
https://www.youtube.com/watch?v=RFDatCchpus

A Parents' Guide to Sex Education - Parenting Tips
https://www.youtube.com/watch?v=-OdOGqUnE60

Advocates for Youth - Sex education overview of research
http://www.advocatesforyouth.org/publications/1487

Parents' Sex Ed Center - http://www.advocatesforyouth.org/parents-sex-ed-center-home

Center for Disease Control starting points
https://www.cdc.gov/healthyyouth/sexualbehaviors/
https://www.cdc.gov/std/life-stages-populations/stdfact-teens.htm

SafelyEverAfter.com - Safety tips for parents and kids

scarleteen.com - Straight talk for teens about sex and sexuality

www.uua.org/re/owl - Unitarian Universalist Lifespan Sexuality Education: Our Whole Lives (OWL)

The Boy's Body Book, Kelli Dunham, Applesauce Press, 4th Edition (July 4, 2017) 9-12 years

The Girl's Body Book, Kelli Dunham, Applesauce Press, 4th Edition (July 4, 2017) 9-12 years

iRules: What Every Tech-Healthy Family Needs to Know about Selfies, Sexting, Gaming, and Growing Up, Janell Burley Hofmann, Rodale Books (May 6, 2014) Parents

I Said No! A Kid-to-Kid Guide to Keeping Private Parts Private, Kimberly King, Zack King, Sue Rama, Boulden Publishing, 3rd Edition (December 1, 2016) 5 and up

It's Not the Stork!: A Book About Girls, Boys, Babies, Bodies, Families and Friends, Robie H. Harris & Michael Emberley, Candlewick, 1st Edition (August 26, 2008)

It's So Amazing!: A Book about Eggs, Sperm, Birth, Babies, and Families, Robie H. Harris & Michael Emberley, Candlewick, 15th Anniversary New Edition (August 8, 2014)

It's Perfectly Normal: Changing Bodies, Growing Up, Sex, and Sexual Health, Robie H. Harris & Michael Emberley, Candlewick, 20th Anniversary New Edition (August 8, 2014) 11 and up

The Lion, The Witch and The Wardrobe, C.S. Lewis, HarperCollins, Reprint Edition (January 2, 2008)

Protecting the Gift: Keeping Children and Teenagers Safe (and Parents Sane), Gavin de Becker, Dell, Reprint Edition (May 9, 2000) Parents

Ready, Set, Grow!: A "What's Happening to My Body?" Book for Girls, Lynda Madaras, Linda Davick, William Morrow Paperbacks, 1st Edition (July 14, 2003) 8-11 years

On Your Mark, Get Set, Grow!: A "What's Happening to My Body?" Book for Boys, Lynda Madaras, Paul Gilligan, William Morrow Paperbacks, 1st Edition (February 13, 2008) 8-10 years

The Safe Side - Internet Safety: A Super-Fun DVD That Helps Cool Kids Stay Safer Online, DVD, G-rated, 5 and up

The Safe Side - Stranger Safety: Hot Tips to Keep Cool Kids Safe With People They Don't Know and Kinda Know, DVD, G-rated, 5 and up

S.E.X.: The All-You-Need-To-Know Sexuality Guide to Get You Through Your Teens and Twenties, Heather Corinna, Da Capo Lifelong Books, 2nd Edition (July 12, 2016) 13 and up

Stick Up for Yourself: Every Kid's Guide to Personal Power and Positive Self-Esteem, Gershen Kaufman, Lev Raphael, Pamela Espeland, Free Spirit Publishing, 2nd Revised Edition (October 15, 1999) 8-12 years

Now For the Good Stuff

What do kids like best
about homeschooling?

"Grown-ups never understand anything by themselves, and it is tiresome for children to be always and forever explaining things to them."

– ANTOINE DE SAINT-EXUPERY, *THE LITTLE PRINCE*

I will let homeschool kids speak for themselves here.

"I can study what I want and still have time to work, sew, learn life skills, cook, help my mom and spend as much time as I want studying and writing and being productive." - Meghan, age 14

"I don't have to sit at a desk all day. I can take lots of breaks to bike and run around outside. And I can learn as fast or as slow as I want; if I learn something really fast I don't have to sit through other people learning it slowly." - Michael, age 13

"You have a lot more free time just to wonder and look stuff up on the internet and learn things." - Benjamin, age 10

"Homeschooling is the worst form of education, except for all the others." - Anonymous, age 18

"The best thing about homeschooling is that it gives us more freedom." - Faith, age 12

"Not having to rush around to stand in lines." - Oliver, age 8

"Being together as a family." - Evelyn, age 10

"I can eat snacks while I'm studying." - Anonymous, age 7

"I can make and mix up [a] schedule that suits my day."
- Anonymous, age 13

"We get to spend so much time together as a family."
- Anonymous

"I love spending time with my family." - JJ, age unknown

Here is what parents have reported are the things the kids like best:

"They can sleep in, and they have a lot of free time to explore their passions."

"No drama that goes along with public school kids."

"Sleeping in. Not being bullied. Having a choice in what he learns (to a point)."

"My kids love pursuing their own education—being accountable and responsible for their own education."

"My youngest would say sleeping in and my oldest would say flexible schedule and hanging out with friends when other kids are in school!"

"Right now she is a fast growing teen and being awake to learn by 7:30 would be very difficult. So flexible learning time and better sleep."

"They have lots of time to play and pursue a variety of lovely things on their time without being rushed."

Our typical homeschooling day...or week

"What is most important and valuable about the home as a base for children's growth into the world is not that it is a better school than the schools, but that it isn't a school at all."

– JOHN HOLT

We don't have a typical day. I'm not even sure we have a typical week. But I will try to give you a rundown of what we generally find ourselves doing during the week. Recently we've instituted a weekly goal-setting time. To make it stick, and make it fun, we walk to the local cafe and eat ice cream Monday mornings before doing homework and talk about what the two older kids want to achieve during the upcoming week and month. We shopped for notebooks for them to write their goals in. Our oldest has a nice leather-bound book embossed with "Master Plan" on the front, which makes him feel like he's plotting something, and our middle boy chose one that says, "Thoughts." After ice cream we go over our ultimate homeschooling goals, talk about what interests them and how we can find resources for them, and schedule time to get everything done that they want to achieve. Sometimes we need to work with specific deadlines, such as projects for a science fair or a music recital, and other times they take something as far as they like before switching to a different topic.

The goals for the week vary for each individual. We make goals about exercise and biking, workbooks, baking cookies, birthday party planning, piano practice, geometry, books to read, computer coding to do, creative projects to make, and interesting subjects to explore. I want them to be excited, and even when something doesn't seem like an academic subject and there might not be that much to get out of it, they often will delve deeply into it and learn all kinds of things that I wasn't expecting.

I talk to them about my personal goals for the week, as well, to show them that adults benefit from the same planning. Modeling behavior that you want them to emulate is a good idea. It also shows them that I'm not just hanging around to remind them to get their own stuff done. I'm getting plenty done myself, even if they're not seeing it. (For example, writing this book in the morning before anyone else is awake, and doing housework while they are glued to the computer doing coding.) After we've decided what to work on for the week, we head back home and get started.

First thing in the morning, after breakfast and chores, before our weekly goal session, is free computer time. The older boys each get half an hour to play games or work on whatever they want. Sometimes the youngest takes a turn as well, but often he is busy working on Legos or an art project or building something outside. I sometimes have to remind them to eat breakfast, because we don't usually get up at the same time.

My kids then spend a few minutes a day (15-60 depending on age and other commitments) working through formal educational work, which also covers some of their fine motor needs. Sometimes that is actual homework from co-op classes they are taking, but not always. We still call it homework, though. We especially like using the Brain Quest workbooks, because they cover a wide range of subjects lightly and are inexpensive. We've used the "Spelling in 10 Minutes a Day" workbooks. Those now appear to be out of print. (I had to order the last one from Amazon's used sellers list and it shipped from England, complete with British spellings.) *Handwriting Without Tears* was much better for learning cursive than the Brain Quest workbook. I wasn't going to bother with cursive at all except to make sure they knew how to do it, but our occupational therapist said that cursive uses different muscles than printing, and is much better at building intrinsic as opposed to extrinsic strength and coordination. We've bought a geometry curriculum for our oldest, and the *Lightning Literature* sets for a couple of years now. We also really like the *Sylvan Learning* math books, and keep one in the car so that our middle son can get some of his formal work done while on the way to activities at least three days a week. Unfortunately the same doesn't work for our oldest, who gets headaches from reading or writing in the car.

Then we have chores, and occupational therapy for the younger two twice a week, which is when our oldest generally makes cookies, practices piano, and works on things that require more concentration and fewer interruptions, like math and literature and programming. He finished up his own occupational therapy last year.

We make sure there is time on the computer for learning, not just playing, although I'm sure it feels like playing to them. It ranges from watching TedEd and other educational videos, doing typing programs, or programming in Scratch, Java or Python, to other creative work like blogging, writing stories, and board game design. Even the youngest has gotten excited about watching his brothers programming in Scratch and has started doing it himself.

During the school year I ask them to do two sets of homework before they have another free computer turn, but in the summer we are more likely to let one set of formal work slide in favor of things like swimming, biking, summer camps, and travel.

But wait, there's more! Yes, we do actually get out of the house and see other people. We've gone on field trips to a fire station, Minnesota Public Radio, local nature centers, and art museums. That's not to mention just going by ourselves to interesting spots, but I mean actual field trips with other homeschoolers. See, we're not hermits! Plus, we have regular groups of homeschoolers we meet with to pursue a variety of interests. We do weekly LARPing (Live Action Role Playing) at a local park and have a monthly club for making board games, a monthly board game playing day (which has some overlap with the last group), and a group that meets monthly for various outings including board games, field trips, Halloween and Pi Day parties, sledding, swimming, and camping. We don't do everything every time, because that would be too much, but we do participate in all of them regularly.

During the academic year our homeschool co-op meets weekly, and there are other classes that we throw in to keep things interesting. Over the years we've done circus classes (we are very lucky that Saint Paul has a great youth circus company, called Circus Juventas), gymnastics, martial arts, ceramics, piano, algebra, swimming, improv theater, and paper and book crafting.

On top of all that we try to take a road trip every year to see at least one of our sets of relatives, who are spread out all over. Travel, broadening our family's perspectives, and keeping in touch with relatives are priorities for us. We set aside some money each month in our travel fund so that we can afford to go interesting places. Generally, driving where we want to go is the least expensive option, especially if we can find places to stay along the way where we can cook dinner and breakfast. We try to see something new each time, even if it's a place we've been before. My dad told me that each time my family went on vacation he noticed that we kids had a learning explosion shortly thereafter, and we've seen the same result with our own kids. Our oldest worked out a slight speech impediment on his own about two weeks after our first big road trip, and curiosity and interest are generally very high during and after a trip.

And yet there are plenty of days when we have time to lounge around the house, for the kids to read or make something, and to become bored and wish we had something planned. How does that happen? Well, it's because we fit most of our activities into the time when everyone else is in school—and still we have time left over. On days when I feel like we hardly accomplished a thing, I can look at a list of our activities or a photo album of the last year, and remind myself that taking days off is actually a good thing.

Finally, we take a day away from all computer screens every week. Sundays we shut down the computer, unplug the wifi, leave the tablet in a drawer, and don't play on the smartphones, and although we do occasionally send texts, we keep it to a minimum. We instituted this policy one New Year's Day, and it took the kids almost a full year to stop complaining about "No Computer Day." Maybe it would have helped if we'd named it "Family Day" or something more positive. I will admit that it took me six months to get used to it myself. I never realized how much of a habit it was for me to just sit down at the computer whenever I wanted to check something or simply when I had a quiet moment. I'm just glad that I got used to screen-free days before I actually had a decent smartphone that I was in the habit of using all the time. My phone was clunky and a bit unreliable, and I mainly used it for emergencies. My husband had a much harder time putting his phone down on Sundays, and I had to keep reminding him that "No Computer Day" was all-inclusive. Now it's a day when we spend more time together as a family, going on outings and playing games and cooking together, or even just reading quietly on the couch, and it's the day that my husband enjoys special time with one of the boys (or me) on a rotating basis.

Even listing all the great things we do doesn't keep me from wondering if I am doing enough. It's very hard not to compare yourself to other families and think they have it all together, or that their style of homeschooling would work better for you if only you could get everyone to sit down and do more formal studies. Every time I try to force the kids into a more rigid structure, though, it doesn't go well. They are self-motivated, which is what we have tried to foster, and imposing learning on them just doesn't work. I have to remind myself frequently that I really am doing enough, that their lives are full and rich and that they know how to learn whatever they will need in the coming years.

TIP: No matter what someone else's homeschooling looks like, yours will look different. Try not to compare yourself to other homeschooling families. Pick and choose ideas that you like, and do your best in your own way.

What would I do differently in retrospect?

"It is easy to be wise after the event."
– SIR **ARTHUR CONAN** DOYLE, *THE COMPLETE SHERLOCK HOLMES*

It's always easier to look back and see where you "should" have done things differently. Give yourself a break, go forward from where you are, and ask veteran homeschoolers what they would have done differently. The more people you talk to, the more likely you are to see patterns in what they suggest, and the more likely you are to find suggestions that resonate with you. It won't be too long before you're that veteran homeschooler with sage advice for those starting out.

The main thing I would have done differently is worry less. Many of my friends will probably be surprised to hear this, because I am generally cheerful and positive about homeschooling and life in general, but in fact I worried a lot. I looked at various research and read a lot of books on learning and development and homeschooling. I met other homeschoolers and went to lectures and seminars. I talked things over with my husband, and we decided how we felt it was best to raise the kids. And then I worried about it. Looking back, there are so many things that either turned out fine or that needed changing and we changed them, and none of it required the level of anxiety that I applied. I could have saved myself a lot of stress. Every so often I remember something my uncle said to me when we were walking through a crowd at the airport. We had passed a family interacting in a way that caught his attention, and he said, "There are a whole lot of different ways to parent, but I've found that by and large we all turn out fine." That helps me to keep some perspective; if we try our best, our kids will most likely turn out fine.

Something else I would have done differently would be keep up my professional networks rather than narrowing my social groups to parents of young children and other homeschoolers. I did try, but this was in the days before Facebook and Linked In, and because we had moved twice (first to Switzerland, then to Saint Paul) it was harder to keep up with people. Our emails slowly petered out. Instead of joining photography groups in Saint Paul and making new connections there, I focused on connecting with parenting and homeschooling groups. Understandable, especially for new parents, but in retrospect I wish I had kept up a little better.

Another thing I would have done differently is to teach more cursive. I didn't see much point in it beyond making sure the kids could read it and form the letters, but it turns out we should have spent more time on it. It would have improved their fine motor control earlier. On the other hand, they willingly did the cursive workbooks for their occupational therapists, whereas I had trouble motivating them to do any cursive before. Maybe that had something to do with my own attitude toward cursive, and also not having a decent workbook. Cursive is often not even taught in schools anymore, which can be a handicap. My mother has beautiful cursive, and in the college biology classes that she teaches she comes across students who can't read her writing. It makes things very difficult for the students trying to read some of her lab exam cards during a test. She has thousands of them that she has written up over the years, and she has no interest in—or time for—typing the cursive ones into a computer.

The other things are more specific to our family. I just wish I had known how fabulous therapists are these days. Both our older boys have benefitted tremendously from a wonderful cognitive-behavior therapist who helped them get tools for anger management and for social anxiety. Unfortunately, it took people outside our family in both cases to notice that what we found worrisome and frustrating was something that was totally treatable. It's hard to be told that your kid needs therapy, and for a long time I tried to learn about social anxiety and do the work myself before I gave in and made an appointment for our oldest. If only I had done so earlier! Within two months he was like a different kid. When our very mellow second son was having trouble flying off the handle frequently, it took a friend of ours mentioning that anger in kids can be a sign of depression before I made an appointment. This time I didn't resist it, although it did take someone outside the family pointing out there was a problem that was treatable. And again, just a few sessions with the therapist did wonders to help him figure out and manage his own feelings.

And finally, along the same lines, I wish I had known how much good occupational therapists can do for kids. We took our oldest in for work on his sensory processing disorder, especially his extreme sensitivity to noise and his very high pain threshold. When they tested him, they found a variety of other things that he needed to work on as well, such as balance and cross-body coordination and fine motor work. Because he climbed everything in sight and rarely fell down, I would never have suspected he had balance issues. I thought his inability to ride a bike was because I didn't encourage him to try often enough. He started therapy in January of his 11th year, and when the snow melted in April he learned to ride his bike within 10 minutes of trying. After he completed his therapy we had both of his brothers tested, and it turned out they had balance and cross-body coordination and fine motor issues, too. We started them at a younger age than their brother. Our middle son took a few days longer to learn to ride his bike, but managed it at age 10, and our youngest may learn it even sooner.

I hope that this quick retrospective will be helpful to new home-schoolers, and to anyone dealing with developmental struggles with their children. I also hope that it will help all parents to relax and get on with what needs to be done without worrying so much. Yes, some-times there are things that need to be worked out, and yes, sometimes we don't recognize them or take care of them as early as could be. You do the best you can with what you know at the time, learn from it and improve. Your kids do the best they can with what they know, and they are learning and improving too. We're all here to learn and grow, and when we do it together it can be a beautiful thing.

TIP: Don't sweat the small stuff! Look at how things are working, make changes when you need to, trust that the kids will turn out fine, and let them know you think they'll turn out fine.

Homeschool parents chime in

"I love knowing my kids in depth, what they think, why they think about things the way they do, having time to discuss and explore life, ideas, perspectives, morals, ethics, world view, etc. I love being with them in real time every day, moving through life, learning organically. I love learning with them, pursuing education together. I love the bond, the love, the strength of our relationships, and growing together."

– JP, HOMESCHOOLING TWO

I took a poll of homeschoolers to see what tips they might have to add to everything I've written, because other homeschoolers often have great ideas. I was surprised to find that almost all the tips fell into six broad categories, which I will summarize for you here. The first three were by far the most popular.

First, relax. You've got this, and if you just do your best the kids will most likely turn out fine. This is the most common tip given to both new homeschoolers and more veteran ones.

"Relax and breathe. Even on your worst days, the kids are still learning something." - Anonymous

"Relax. Take a breath and play. Enjoy your kids while they're young and don't sweat the academic stuff until [later]. They learn so much more than you realize through play." - Deb, homeschooling one

Second, trust yourself and your kids. This can be hard to do in a culture that tells us that teachers know best how and what we should learn, and sometimes learning to trust ourselves can be the most beneficial lesson in homeschooling.

"Ask for suggestions and look at all the information out there, but in the end, ignore everyone else and do what feels right to you." - Nic, homeschooling one

"Trust your child's innate curiosity to drive their most valuable and meaningful learning. In other words, get your agenda out of the way." - Hannah, homeschooling two

Third, don't try to recreate school at home. There is so much more freedom around learning when you're not trying to do it the way everyone else is. Create together what will best serve you and your family.

"You don't have to imitate the public-school model. Kids learn. Personally, as long as his annual test shows about a year of progress, I don't get too concerned." - Gina, homeschooling one with special needs

"You don't have to make YOUR homeschool look like a school or anyone else's homeschool. It has to work for you and your family." - Joy, homeschooling three

Fourth, focus on the future. This will help you keep your equilibrium and balance. What are your long-term goals for your kids and yourself? Look at goals beyond getting through this year's curriculum, or even to have the kids graduate eventually. What kind of people would you like them to be when they are adults? What kind of relationship would you like to have with them?

"Take the long-term view. Write down your overall goals —why you are homeschooling—and take it out to look at when you are anxious or worried." - Ann, homeschooled two, both now graduated

"The best advice I ever received was to make a list of 10 things you want your child to learn by the time they are an adult. Doing this gives you perspective on what matters most and gives you something to return to when the going gets tough. Like everything, homeschool will have ups and downs." - Anonymous

Fifth, be flexible. Rarely will things go exactly the way we envision them. Getting too attached to a particular curriculum or outcome or schedule can be stressful for both parents and children. Being ready to change directions when necessary will smooth the whole process.

"Remember that what works for one child may not work for another. Also, what will work one year for your child may not work the second. Always be prepared to change, and to be flexible."
- Brandie, homeschooling two

"When kids are having a hard day, stop to love them. Read a book, go on an outing, have one-on-one time. Relationships are important." - Sarah, homeschooling two

Sixth, do your research. Know your local homeschooling laws, know what resources are out there and where to find them, know how your kids learn and interact best, and don't be afraid to ask other people for help.

"Research, research, research. But don't get swallowed up in homeschooling. Remember to take care of yourself, too." - Nina, homeschooling one

Resources and References

And the Skylark Sings with Me - Adventures in Homeschooling and Community-Based Education, David H. Albert, New Society Publishers, 1st Paperback Edition (September 27, 1999)

The Book of Learning and Forgetting, Frank Smith, Teachers College Press (May 1, 1998)

Homeschool Your Child for Free: More than 1,400 Smart, Effective, and Practical Resources for Educating Your Family at Home, Laura Maery Gold & Joan M. Zielinsky, Three Rivers Press, 2nd Updated, Revised Edition (August 4, 2009)

Playful Parenting: An Exciting New Approach to Raising Children That Will Help You Nurture Close Connections, Solve Behavior Problems, and Encourage Confidence, Lawrence J. Cohen, Ballantine Books, Reprint Edition (April 30, 2002)

Raising Freethinkers: A Practical Guide for Parenting Beyond Belief, Dale McGowan, Molleen Matsumura, Amanda Metskas, Jan Devor, AMACOM (February 11, 2009)

The Teenage Liberation Handbook: How to Quit School and Get a Real Life and Education, Grace Llewellyn, Lowry House Publishers, Revised Expanded Edition (September 1, 1998)

The Ultimate Book of Homeschooling Ideas: 500+ Fun and Creative Learning Activities for Kids Ages 3-12, Linda Dobson, Three Rivers Press, 1st Edition (November 26, 2002)

Final Note

As you can see, homeschoolers are generally not hermits, and the opportunities to be part of your community are largely dependent on you and your ability to reach out and find them. Make sure to keep up your family's current friendships while making new ones in the homeschool community. If you tend toward introversion you may need to make a special effort to keep yourself and your kids involved in the community. Some states, like Pennsylvania, have social structures to support homeschoolers, but in many cases it's incumbent upon the families themselves to locate what they need. It's worth the effort to make new friendships in the homeschool community while keeping up with the old ones, so get out and be social to the extent that it suits your family. Our family has both introverts and extroverts, and we find ways to get everyone what they need. It just requires a little extra thought and planning. My husband is often happy to stay home and get the downtime he needs while rest of us go to social gatherings, or he may leave early with our oldest son while the younger two and I get extra social time. Remember, too, that while homeschool groups can be great, if you can't find one that suits you, a few close friends might fit the bill just fine.

Homeschooling also doesn't require staying at home slaving over schoolbooks all day. It doesn't even require stuffing as much information as you can into your kids. That is an important point to remember: you don't have to teach your kids everything right now, nor provide your kids with every opportunity every time. It's the cumulative effect over a period of years that makes the difference, whether they are at home or in school. Giving your kids a context in which to put the information they are learning, and showing them how to find what they want to learn, will go a long way toward setting them on a path of lifelong learning. Our kids laugh when people ask if they get summer vacation, because they know that learning never stops. Vacation *is* learning for us, just one of the ways that we make homeschooling fun.

Being mindful and intentional when working with your kids will help smooth out the rough edges in daily life. If there's been friction in the family around schoolwork or chores, bringing the three rules of mindful parenting (assess, pause, listen) to the discussion can be a good way to discover what's going on underneath the surface to cause that friction. Being present and receptive to what's working and what isn't working will help you be flexible and work with rather than against your kids' needs and natural tendencies. And paying attention to your own needs and taking some down time will help you to keep your perspective and your temper when it's been a long day.

You don't have to be the perfect homeschooling parent to make homeschooling work for you and your family. None of us are perfect and there's plenty of us who are making homeschooling work. You don't even have to be dedicated to homeschooling as a way of life. Plenty of people find that conventional school works some of the time for some of their kids. You just have to take a good look at the options and be flexible enough to choose the ones that work for your family, even if they're not how other people are educating their children. If homeschooling is the option that works best for your family, then welcome to homeschooling! The challenges are well worth the rewards.

ABOUT THE AUTHOR:

Kathy Oaks is a photographer and educator who is passionate about travel and education and is dedicated to helping parents and kids who want to take a non-traditional approach to education. Kathy wrote *Homeschoolers Are Not Hermits* to support families as they make the transition from conventional schooling to something completely different, bringing fun, mindfulness and flexibility to the adventure of homeschooling. She is currently working on a resource guide companion to this book.

You can read her blog at <u>HomeschoolersNotHermits.com</u> and please get your free resource kit for homeschooling and road trips at <u>HomeschoolersNotHermits.com/book</u>

Photo by Kelle Green

CPSIA information can be obtained
at www.ICGtesting.com
Printed in the USA
BVHW032011270820
587487BV00002B/649